S0-BJK-173

The Art of Go Series:

Volume Two

Capturing Stones

Wu Dingyuan and Yu Xing
Editor – Everett Thiele

Originally published by the People's Athletic
Publishing Co., China, under the title of Measures
Following Capture

All rights reserved according to international law. This book and any parts thereof may not be reproduced in print or electronically without written permission from the publisher.

ISBN 1 - 889554 - 17 - 0

Editing, layout, and diagrams by Everett Thiele
Proof Assistance - David Dows, John Lamping, and Steve Plate
Translated by Dr. Sidney W.K. Yuan

And it came to pass at midnight that the LORD struck all the firstborn in the land of Egypt, from the firstborn of Pharaoh who sat on his throne to the firstborn of the *captive* who was in the dungeon, and all the firstborn of livestock.

Exodus 12:29

Yutopian Enterprises
2255 29th Street, Suite 3
Santa Monica, CA 90405 USA
1-800-988-6463
Email: sales@yutopian.com
Web Page: http://www.yutopian.com

1 2 3 4 5 6 7 8 9 10

Table of Contents

Preface

In go there are various capturing techniques which require sacrificing stones. Most beginners fail to see these moves. Even advanced players might overlook them if they don't pay attention. Mastering these techniques equips a player with powerful weapons for both attack and defense. In addition, the training in visualization that we get by studying these tactical finesses will serve us in good stead even in more straightforward positions.

Generally, there are the following three kinds of sacrifice techniques, each of which is devoted a chapter:

1) Under the Stones (Ishi-no-shita)- This spectacular technique involves allowing your opponent to make a seemingly decisive capture in order to set up a recapture, thereby forming an eye, taking territory or forcing ko.

2) Killing Oversized Eyes (Nakade)- With this technique you also sacrifice some stones in order to then make a placement at the vital point inside the resulting oversized eye. In most cases this reduces the nakade to only one eye, but in certain positions you can convert the whole nakade into a single false eye. You are no doubt familiar with such unsettled shapes as the pyramid-four, bulky-five and flowery-six. However, if the defender's position has certain defects, you can even sacrifice larger shapes which are related to these basic patterns.

3) Other Sacrifice Techniques- Concerning various ways of using throw-ins to force your opponent into shortage of liberties or make false eyes.

This book provides thorough training in the three types of techniques listed above. By working through the following reading problems, you can practice these skills and improve your level of play.

Chapter 1
Under the stones (Ishi-no-shita)

Problem 1
Black to play

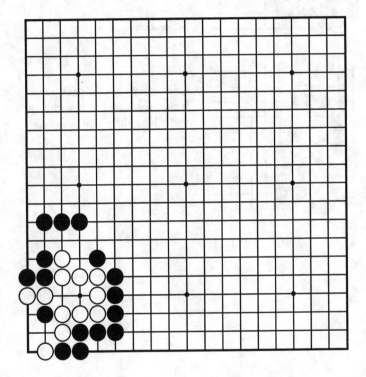

Can Black kill this white corner group?

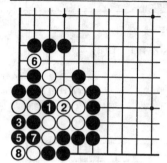

Correct Answer- Black's throw-in and atari at 1 and 3 force White to connect and lose an eye. Black then turns at 5, letting White capture three black stones by wedging in at 6. Black feeds one more stone at 7, and if White resists by capturing with 8...

White 4 connects at 1

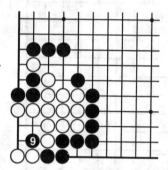

Continuation- ...Black takes two white stones with 9, breaking the eye and killing the group.

Problem 2
White to play

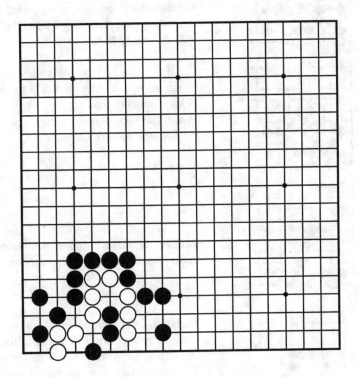

Can the surrounded white
stones make life?

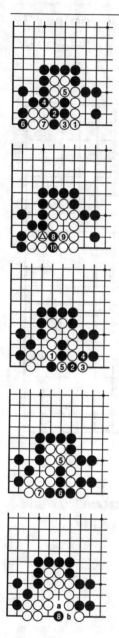

Correct Answer- The descent to white 1 is a calculated move. Black tries to create an under-the-stones shape with black 2. Everything goes according to Black's plan with the moves from 3 to 7.

Continuation- Black plays atari at 8. White plays a counter-atari at 9 forcing Black to capture the four stones with 10. White can then make a second eye by playing in at the marked stone.

11 at the marked stone

Failure- White 1 is not a well thought-out move. Black gets a ko with the moves to 5.

Variation- If white 5 in the previous diagram is played instead as an atari, Black connects at 6. After White captures the five stones with 7, an oversized eye is formed.

Continuation- The placement of 8 makes miai of a and b, so White is dead.

Problem 3
Black to play

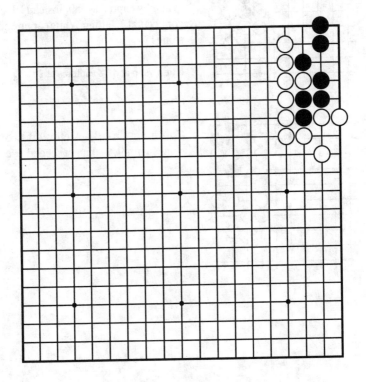

How can the black group
in the corner make life?

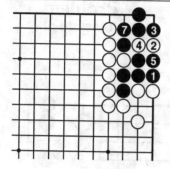

Correct Answer- Black has no choice but to widen his eye space with 1, and block at 3, making an eye. White expects Black to respond to the throw-in at 6 by capturing, but instead Black connects at 7, letting White capture six stones.

6 throws in at 4, 8 captures at 2

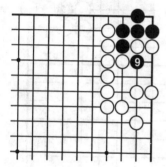

Continuation- Black clips off two stones with 9, making a second eye.

Problem 4
White to play

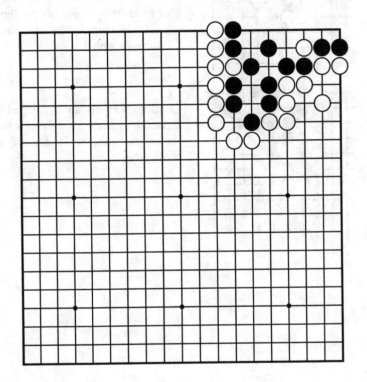

At first glance, Black looks alive. However, White can kill by playing under the stones.

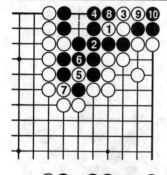

Correct Answer- The atari at white 1 is inevitable, but the descent to white 3 is an exquisite play, forcing Black to descend to 4. White then destroys an eye with 5 and Black is dead. If Black tries to resist by capturing the three white stones with 8, White increases the sacrifice with 9.

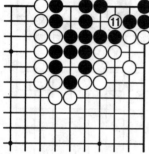

Continuation- Black has hoped to make life by capturing the four white stones, but white 11 finishes off the entire group.

Problem 5
Black to play

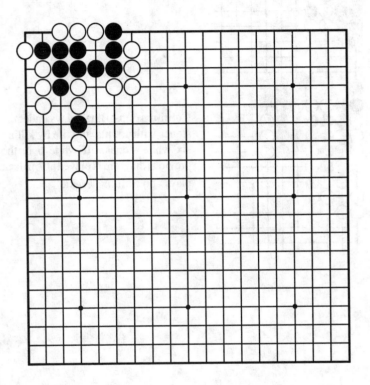

It looks like Black only has one eye in the corner. How should Black play in order to live?

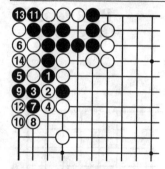

Correct Answer- Black thrusts at 1 and plays atari at 3. White 2 and 4 are forced. With the moves from 5 to 14, White captures four black stones.

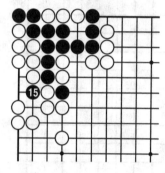

Continuation- Black plays under the stones with 15, making life by killing six white stones. If white 6 in the previous diagram is played at 7, Black plays at 6 forming a seki.

Problem 6
White to play

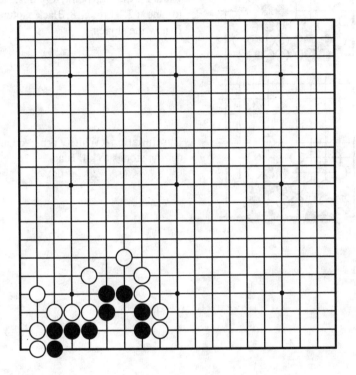

How can White make use
of the under-the-stones
technique to kill Black?

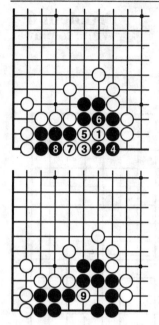

Correct Answer- The attachment at white 1 is the vital point, forcing Black to hane at 2. Through 8, Black captures four white stones.

Continuation- White 9 is played under the stones to kill Black.

Problem 7
White to play

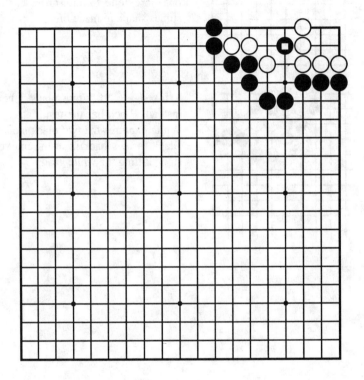

Black is gambling that White won't know how to parry the marked tricky placement. White has to play under the stones to live.

17

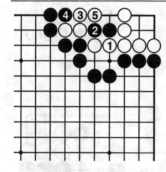

Correct Answer- The connection at white 1 and the cut at black 2 are both necessary. White 3 is a tesuji. When Black plays atari with 4, White feeds one more stone, forming an under-the-stones shape to make life.

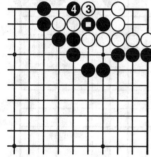

Tricked- If White plays 3 here instead, Black has the tesuji at 4. If White captures the two black stones, Black throws back in at the marked stone killing the white group.

Problem 8
Black to play

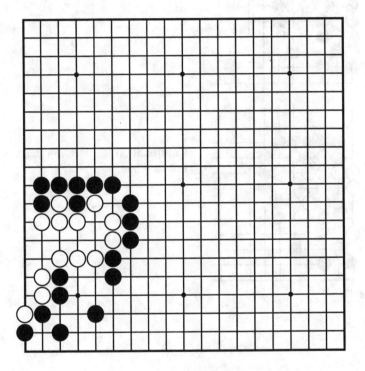

This doesn't look like an easy group to kill, but with a little imagination and thought it can be done. White may have abundant eye space, but there are some glaring weak points to aim at.

19

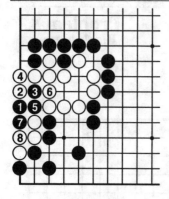

Correct Answer- The placement of black 1 is at the vital point. The subsequent moves are White's strongest defence, but after the capture with white 8...

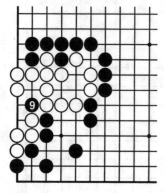

Continuation- ...Black can atari at 9, killing White.

Problem 9
White to play

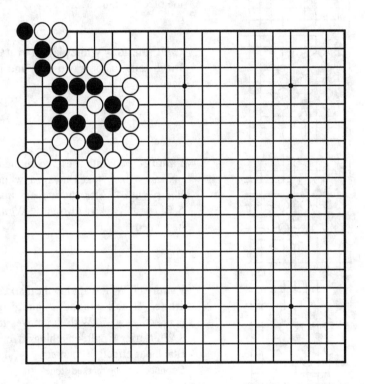

There are some unsettling defects in Black's shape. The question is: how can White take advantage of them?

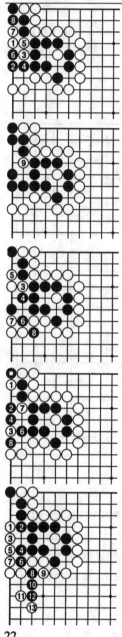

Correct Answer- White 1 occupies the vital point. If Black blocks at 2, White plays a diagonal move at 3. The connection at black 4 is forced. White feeds in stones with 5 and 7, allowing the black capture at 8.

Continuation- White plays atari at 9. Black fails to form two eyes and is dead.

Failure- If White uses 3 to cut here instead, Black takes away a white liberty with 4. After the atari at white 5, Black starts a ko with 6 and 8. White has failed.

Failure- If White captures the marked stone, Black makes a hanging connection at 2. With the moves to 8, White tries to pull something off, but Black has effective counters.
5 connects at the marked stone

Variation- If Black connects at 2 in reply to White's placement at 1, White draws back to 3. Resisting with 4 to 12 is futile. After the hane of white 13, it is all too clear that Black has failed.

Problem 10
White to play

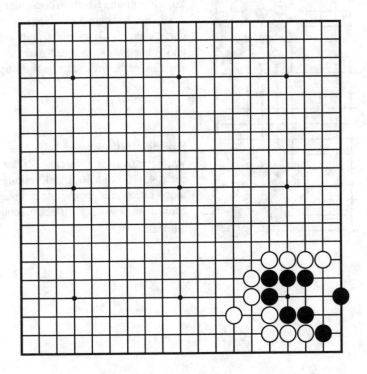

At first glance Black looks alive. What's the best result White can get?

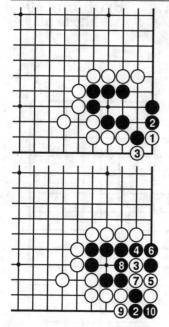

Correct Answer- White can force a ko, while giving Black an opportunity to slip up. The clamp of white 1 is the correct move. Black plays atari at 2 and White plays a counter-atari starting a ko for the life of the black group.

Suicide- If Black resists with 2 here, white jumps in at 3, forcing Black to cut at 4. Through 10, Black captures four white stones, but White can play back in at 7 killing Black unconditionally.

Problem 11
White to play

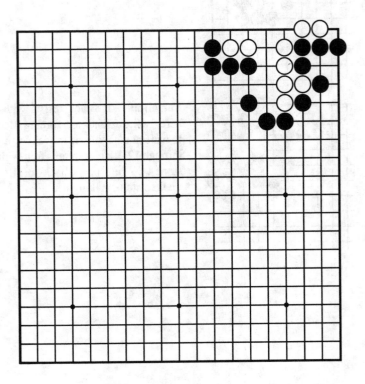

The white group in the corner only seems to have one eye. Is there some way to make life?

25

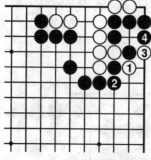

Correct Answer- White ataris at 1 and 3. Black can start a ko with 4 for the life of the white group.

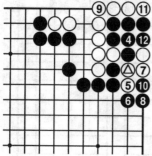

Variation- If Black resists with 4 here, White extends to 5 forcing Black to hane at 6. With the moves from 7 through 12, Black captures four white stones. White plays back in at the marked stone making life.

Problem 12
Black to play

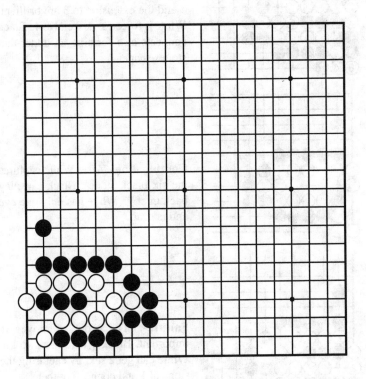

What measures should Black adopt to kill White?

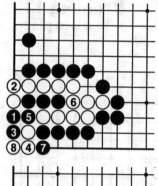

Correct Answer- The atari of black 1 and the extension to 3 are brilliant. White is forced to descend to 4. Black connects at 5 forming an under-the-stones shape.

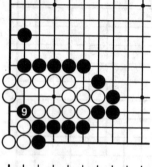

Continuation- After White captures the six black stones, Black can play back in at 9. White has only one eye and is dead.

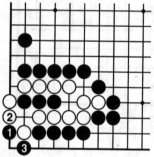

Failure- The order of moves is important. Black 1 here leads to ko. White can get a seki by capturing the stone at 1 and connecting there.

Problem 13
Black to play

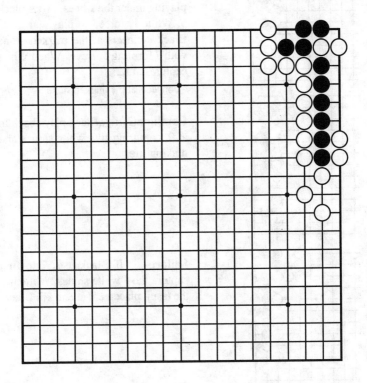

Can Black make life in the corner? Although it may look hopeless, one can apply the under-the-stones technique.

29

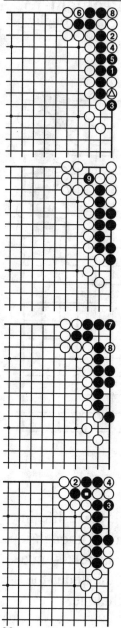

Correct Answer- Black plays atari at 1. White turns at 2 and Black captures at 3. By extending to 4, White overlooks the possibility of Black playing under the stones. After black 5, White is forced to play atari at 6. Black connects at the marked stone with 7 forming one eye. When White captures at 8...

7 connects at the marked stone

Continuation- ...Black plays back in at 9, capturing five white stones and making life.

Failure- If Black uses 7 to first capture the 4 white stones, White has the tesuji placement at 8 to kill Black.

Variation- If White plays atari at 2 instead, Black forms an eye at 3 while reducing White's liberties. For White to capture with 4 is futile, as Black can play back in at the marked stone.

Problem 14
White to play

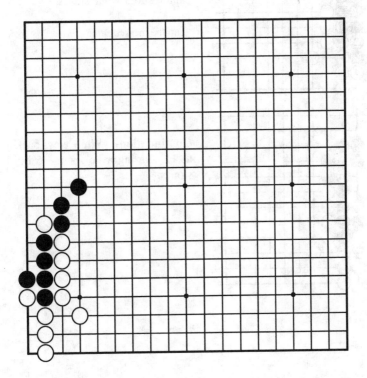

Can White can make a
nuisance of the single
stone behind Black's
lines?

31

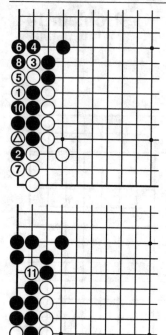

Correct Answer- With the moves from 1 to 5 White forms an under-the-stones shape. Through 10, Black captures four white stones.

9 at the marked stone

Continuation- White plays back in at 11, starting a ko for the 6 black stones.

Problem 15
Black to play

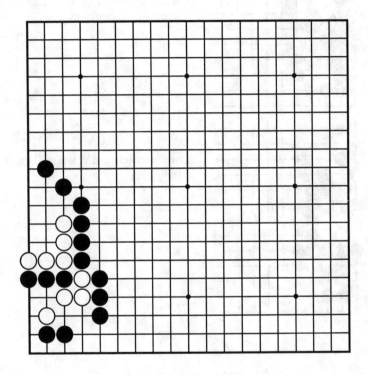

Despite the appearance that White is alive on the left, Black can still kill this group.

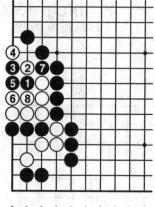

Correct Answer- Black first attaches at 1. The block at white 2 is forced. Black 3 and 5 set up a clever sacrifice. After White captures with 8...

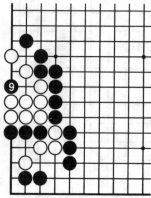

Continuation- ...Black plays in at 9, killing White.

Problem 16
White to play

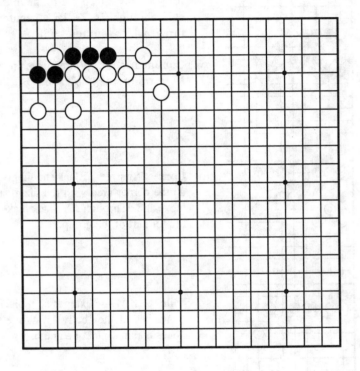

What happens if the lone
white stone in the corner
is set into motion?

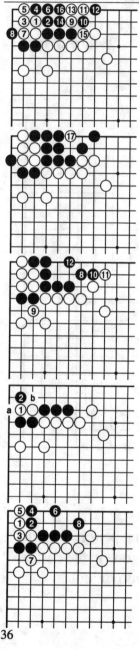

Tricked- White 1 sets a trap for Black. Black blocks at 2. When White turns at 3, Black hanes at 4. White hanes as well. When Black connects at 6, White forms a bulky-five with 7. Black falls for White's trap with the hane at 8. Through 16, Black captures three white stones, but...

Continuation- ...White plays in at 17 turning the tables on Black.

Correct Answer- Black should give up the corner area with the diagonal move at 8. Through 12, Black makes life for part of the group.

Failure- If White extends at 1, black 2 attaches at the 'belly' of White's stones making miai of a and b.

Also Correct- The diagonal play at 1 also takes the corner but is lacking in guile. With the moves up to 8, Black makes life for part of the group.

Problem 17
White to play

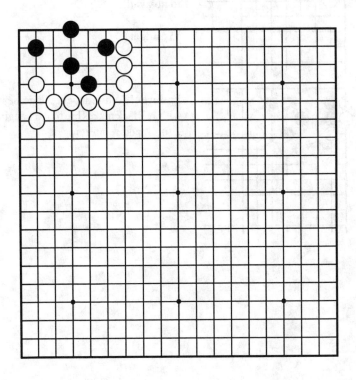

It looks as if Black has ample eye space in the corner. Let's see how White proceeds to kill Black.

37

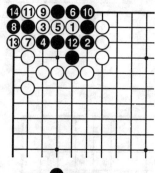

Correct Answer- White clamps at 1 before hopping to 3 and connecting at 5. These are calculated moves. The cut at white 7 is crucial. Through 14, Black captures five white stones, but to no avail.

15 ataris at 3

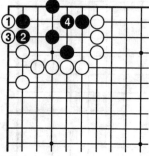

Failure- If White attaches underneath with 1, Black makes life by exchanging 2 for 3, and reinforcing at 4.

38

Problem 18
White to play

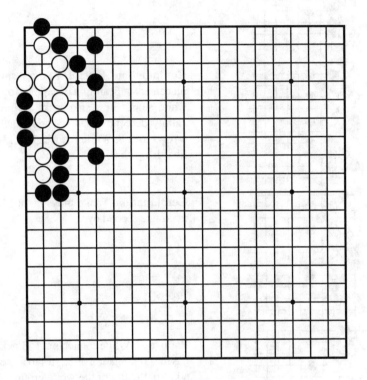

Without careful conside-
ration, White might not
live here.

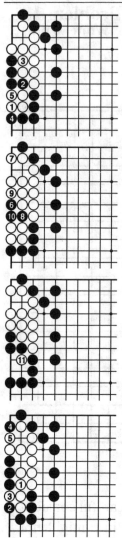

Correct Answer- The descent to white 1 is exquisite. Black cuts at 2 and White plays atari at 3. Through 5, White captures 4 black stones.

Continuation- Black tries the tesuji placement at 6, aiming to capture four white stones in a snapback. White calmly descends to 7. When Black throws in at 8, White reduces Black's liberties with 9.

Continuation- White plays in at 11, making a second eye.

Failure- If White connects at 1, Black has the combination of 2 and 4 to force a ko for the life of the white group.

Problem 19
White to play

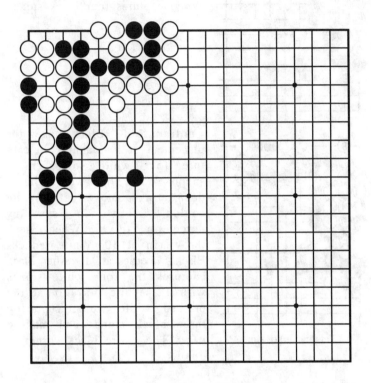

Can White win the battle
in the corner?

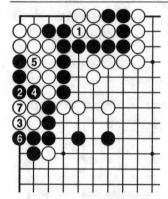

Correct Answer- White forms a bulky-five with 1, reducing Black to only one eye. This is a calculated move. Through 7, White captures four black stones.

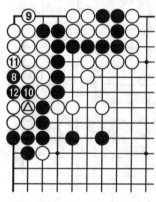

13 at the marked stone

Continuation- Black makes the placement at 8, planning to capture four white stones in a snapback. This would be a devastating move if White couldn't form an eye by descending to 9. When Black throws in at 10, White reduces Black's liberties at 11. After Black captures the four white stones with 12, White plays in at the marked white stone, capturing three black stones and making life. The entire black corner is dead.

Problem 20
Black to play

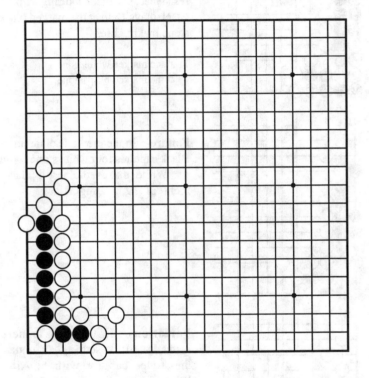

It seems trivial for Black to make life in the corner. However, one little slip-up and Black might be in for a nasty surprise.

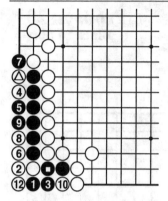

Correct Answer- The atari at black 1 is inevitable. After White's extension to 2, the connection at 3 is a well thought-out move. White puts up stiff resistance, but after capturing with 12, Black plays 13 in at the marked black stone making life.

11 at the marked white stone
13 at the marked black stone

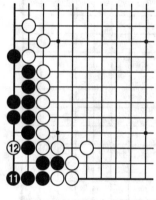

Failure- In the previous diagram, if Black captures four white stones with 11, White makes the tesuji placement of 12, killing Black.

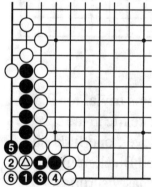

Variation- If white 4 is here instead. Black sets up an under-the-stones capture with 5. After White captures at 6, Black plays in at the marked black stone. (Also, if Black plays 3 at 5, White kills with white 3, black 6, white throw-in at the marked white stone, black 2, white 4.)

Problem 21
White to play

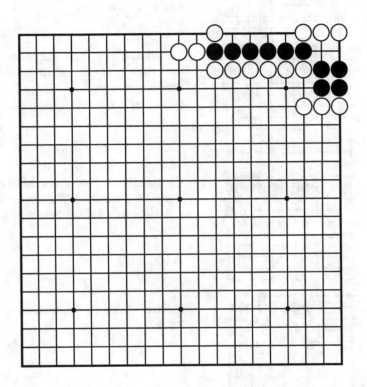

Can White pull anything
off in the corner?

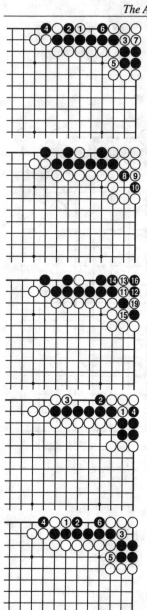

Correct Answer - White must exchange 1 for 2 before cutting at 3. Black is short of liberties and must capture a stone with 4. Through 7, White captures four black stones.

Continuation- Black ataris under the stones at 8. White feeds one more stone at 9. Black captures six white stones.

Continuation- Cutting immediately at white 11 is exquisite. White sqeezes, and through 19 forces Black into a ko fight.

17 at 11   18 at 13

Failure- White 1 here fails to kill Black.

Failure- This white 1 doesn't work either.

Problem 22
White to play

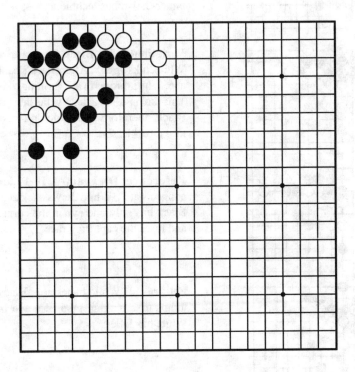

How can White rescue the the eight surrounded stones?

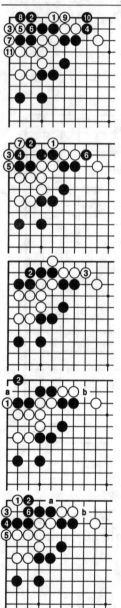

Answer- White hanes at 1 to probe Black's response. Against the hanging connection at 2, white 3 is an effective play. Through 11, White captures some black stones and makes life using the under-the-stones technique.

Variation- If Black blocks at 4, White links up at 5. After Black's hane at 6, White throws in at 7 forming a ko. This ko is also a heavy burden on Black, therefore one shouldn't rush into it recklessly.

Reference Diagram- If Black connects at 2, White draws back at 3. Black has only one eye in the corner and loses the capturing race.

Failure- If White hanes at 1, Black jumps to 2 making miai of a and b. White has failed.

Failure- White tries the placement at 1 instead. Black blocks at 2 and White makes a diagonal move. Both sides block at 4 and 5 respectively. The black connection at 6 makes miai of 'a' and 'b', so White collapses.

Problem 23
White to play

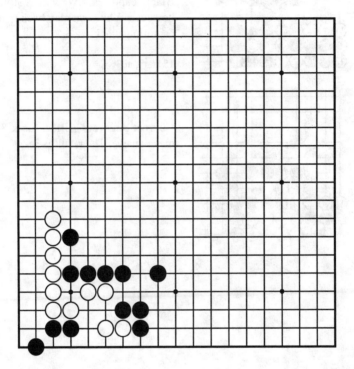

Can White kill the black corner group? Although it looks quite impossible, White might be able to do it using the under-the-stones technique.

49

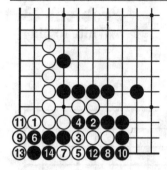

Black Tricked- White 1 prevents Black from making two eyes in the corner. Black is forced to cut off some white stones with 2 and 4. Through 14, Black captures five white stones, however, White can play back in at 3 capturing Black.

15 ataris at 3

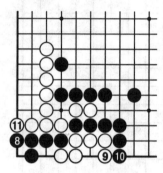

Correct Answer- Black uses 8 to make an eye. The result is seki.

Problem 24
Black to play

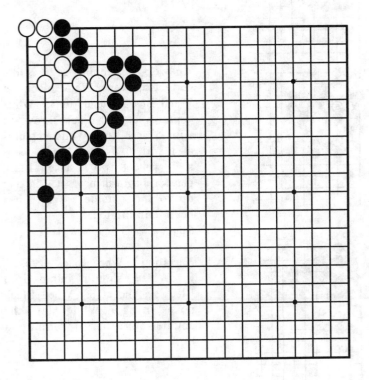

Although White has ample eye space in the corner, Black can still kill. The question is: how?

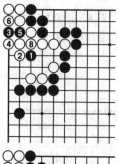

Failure- Black peeps at 1 and White extends to 2. Through white 8, White lives in the corner by forming an under-the-stones shape.

7 at 5

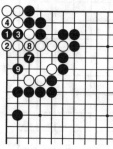

Answer- Peeping at 1 is the correct answer. White blocks at 2 and Black extends to 3. White captures at 4. Black throws-in with 5 at 3, and White captures at 1 with 6. When Black peeps at 7, white 8 is a mistake. Black plays a diagonal move at 9 linking up to the outside. White has been annihilated.

5 throws in at 3   6 captures at 1

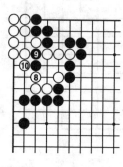

Variation- When Black peeps at 7, White should bump into Black's stone at 8. When Black pokes in at 9, White plays the counter-atari of 10 forming a ko.

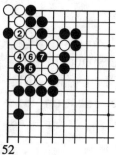

Variation- If White connects at 2 in reply to black 1, Black jumps in at 3. White bumps into the black stone at 4 and Black extends to 5. When White blocks at 6, Black plays the severe move at 7 killing White.

Problem 25
White to play

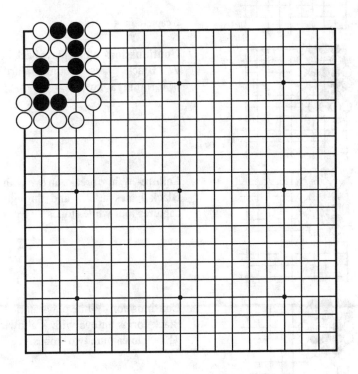

What is White's strongest attack?

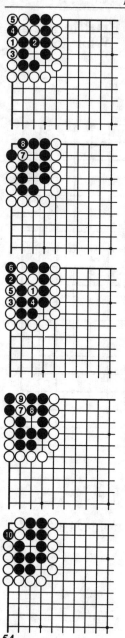

Correct Answer- White hanes at 1 and connects at 3 with a well thought-out plan. When Black throws in at 4, White captures at 5, allowing Black to capture four stones in a snapback.

6 captures at 4

Continuation- White plays back in at 7. Black plays counter-atari at 8 forming a ko.

Failure- White breaks an eye with 1. Black hanes at 2, and through 6 captures four white stones.

Continuation- White plays atari at 7. Black forms an eye with 8 allowing white 9 to capture two stones.

Continuation- Black throws in at 10 making life for the group with a snapback.

Problem 26
Black to play

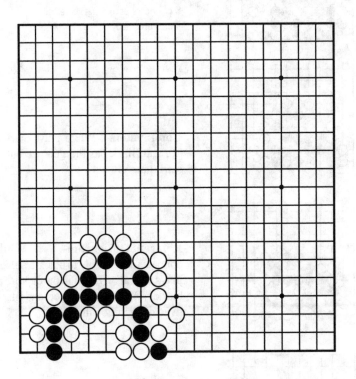

How can Black make life
for his surrounded group?

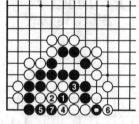

Correct Answer- Black 1 is very clever. White plays atari at 2 and Black squeezes with 3 through 7. White can't connect at 1, so Black captures.

8 connects at the marked stone
9 captures at 1

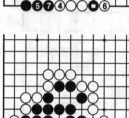

Continuation- White plays atari at 10, and Black has little choice but to start the ko.

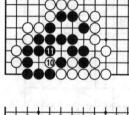

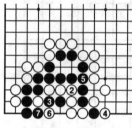

Reference Diagram- If White connects at 2 in reply to black 1. Black plays atari at 3. Through the capture at black 7, White can't connect and Black lives unconditionally.

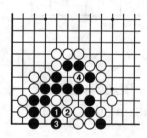

Failure- If Black plays atari at 1 here instead, White plays a counter-atari at 2. The throw-in at 4 puts an end to black's misery.

Problem 27
White to play

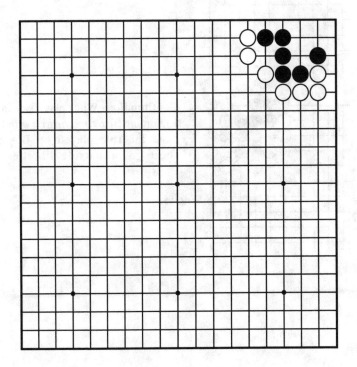

What's the status of the
black corner?

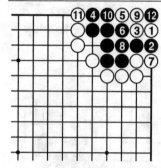

Correct Answer- White 1 is an exquisite placement. Black blocks at 2 and White extends to 3. Through 12, Black captures four white stones.

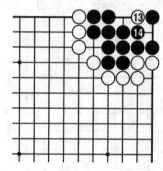

Continuation- White plays back in at 13, forcing Black to form a ko with 14. Note the role played by Black's shortage of outside liberties.

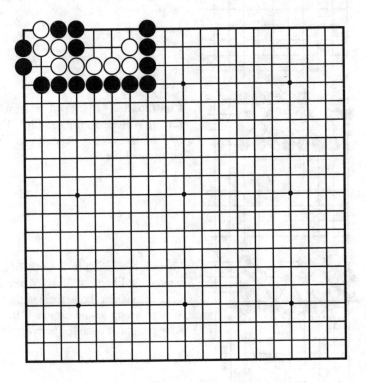

Is the white group dead
or alive?

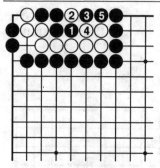

Correct Answer- The extension at black 1 is sharp. After White throws in at 2, Black captures at 3 and connects at 5, allowing White to capture four stones with 6.

6 captures at 2

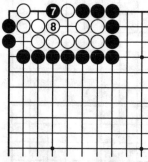

Continuation- Black plays atari at 7, forcing White to form a ko with 8. The fate of the corner depends on the outcome of the ko.

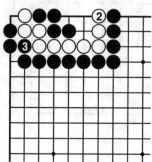

Variation- If white 2 here, Black removes a liberty at 3 and White is dead. Consider how the status of White's group would change if there were one more outside liberty.

60

Problem 29
White to play

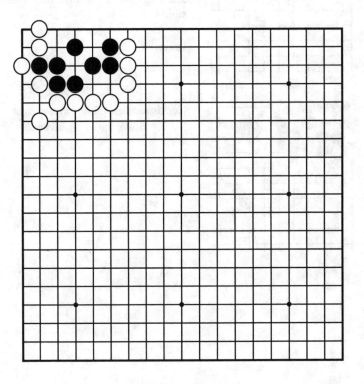

What's the status of this
black group?

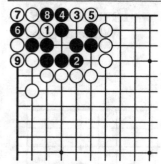

Correct Answer- The turn at 1 and placement at 3 reduce Black to one eye. Up to the connection at White 9, an under-the-stones shape is formed. Although Black captures four White stones...

10 captures at 6

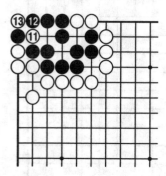

Continuation- White plays atari at 11 forcing Black into a disadvantageous ko.

62

Problem 30
Black to play

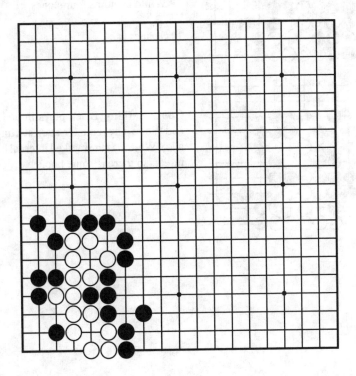

How healthy is this white group?

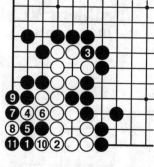

Correct Answer- Black plays at 1 threatening to throw in at 2. This is an exquisite move. If White connects, Black breaks an eye with 3. Through 12 White captures four stones.

12 captures at 8

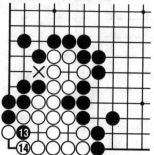

Continuation- Black plays in at 13 and White plays counter-atari, starting a ko. White has the marked internal ko threat, so there is some hope.

Problem 31
Black to play

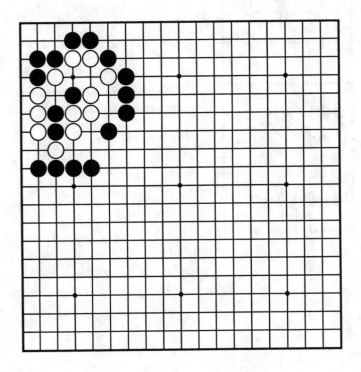

Is is possible to cause any trouble inside the white group?

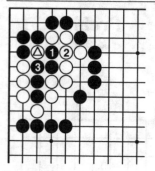

Correct Answer- Black plays atari at 1 and captures at 3, allowing White to capture five Black stones in a snapback.

4 captures at the marked stone

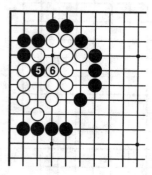

Continuation- Black plays atari at 5, forcing White to form a ko with 6.

Problem 32
Black to play

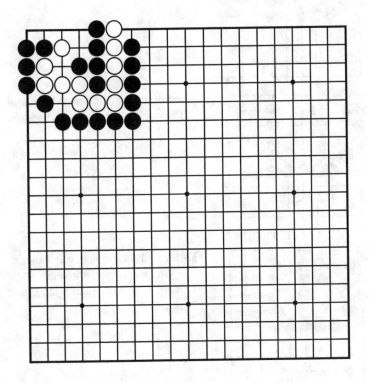

What will be the outcome of the capturing race in the corner?

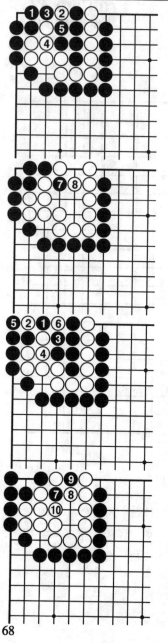

Correct Answer- The descent to Black 1 is a calm move. White has only the diagonal move at 2. Through 6, White captures six stones.

6 captures at 2

Continuation- Black plays back in at 7, forcing White to form a ko with 8.

Failure- Black impulsively hanes at 1. White can now throw in at 2. Through 6, White captures six Black stones.

Continuation- Playing in at 7 no longer works. When White plays atari at 8 and 10, Black cannot connect. Black has failed.

Chapter 2
Oversized Eyes (Nakade)

Problem 33
Black to play

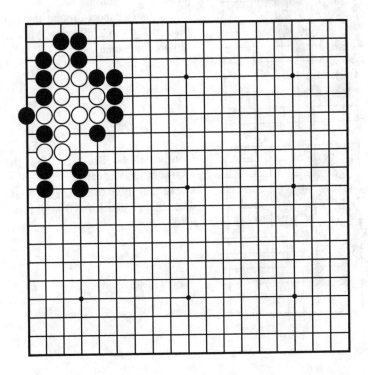

Kill the white group
mercilessly.

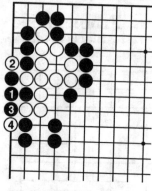

Correct Answer- The connection at 1 is very clever. White throws-in at 2, planning to catch the black stones if they try to connect around the top. Black dodges to 3, allowing White to capture four stones.

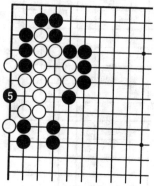

Continuation- Black occupies the vital point at 5 and can extend to either side turning this into a false eye. White dies. Playing black 1 at 3 would start a ko.

Problem 34
White to play

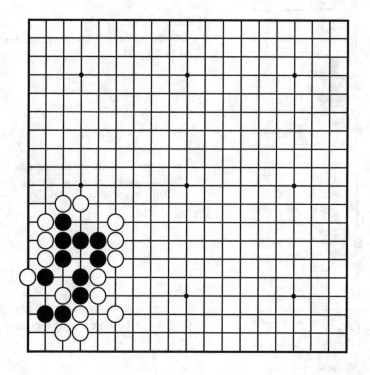

What's the status of the black group?

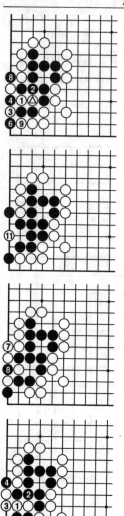

Correct Answer- White plays atari at 1 before the hane at 3. These are well thought-out moves. Through 10, Black captures four white stones.

5 captures at 1   7 connects at 4
10 captures at the marked stone

Continuation- The white placement at 11 kills Black.

Failure- If white 7 connects on the outside, Black captures at 8 starting a ko. White has failed.

Failure- If White connects at 3, Black throws in at 4 making life by capturing four white stones.

Problem 35
Black to play

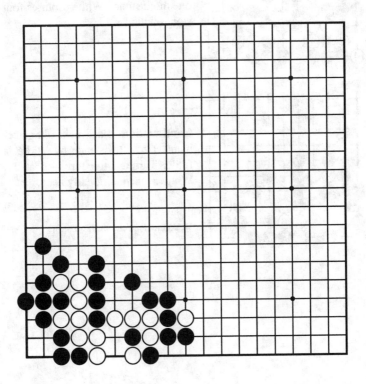

Is the white group alive?

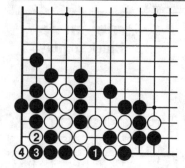

Correct Answer- The capture at black 1 is inevitable. When White plays atari at 2, Black cleverly feeds one more stone. White captures four stones with 4.

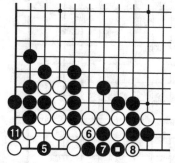

Continuation- Black makes the placement at 5. Resistance by White is futile. Through the throw-in at 11, White is unconditionally dead.

9 plays in at 7
10 connects at the marked stone

Problem 36
Black to play

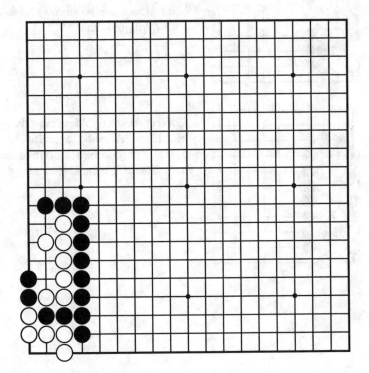

How's the well-being of
the white group?

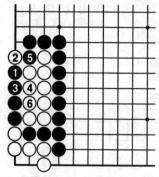

White Fails- The attachment of black 1 strikes the vital point. The atari of white 2 is a mistake. Black links up at 3. Through 6 White captures four black stones. Black throws-in at 1 with 7, killing White.

7 throws-in at 1

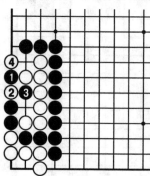

Correct Answer- White must throw in at 2 here. After the capture at black 3, White plays hane at 4. White can make life in the corner by winning the ko.

Problem 37
Black to play

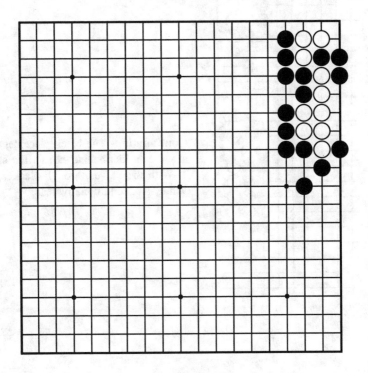

Can the white group with-
stand a black attack?

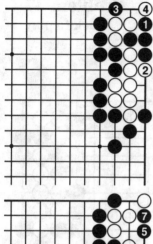

Correct Answer- The extension to black 1 is exquisite. When White plays atari at 2, Black hanes at 3, allowing White to capture four stones at 4.

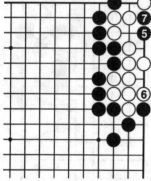

Continuation- The black placement at 5 was the idea behind the sacrifice at 1. With the moves through black 7, White is unconditionally dead.

Problem 38
White to play

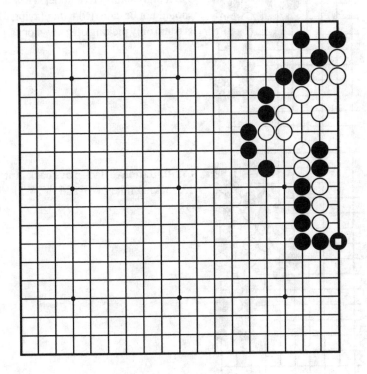

It looks like White has enough eye space to make life, but Black can still kill. The descent of the marked black stone is very effective.

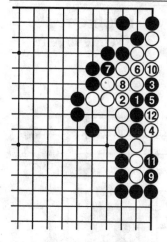

Correct Answer- The extension to black 1 is a sharp play. After white 2 and 4, Black keeps up the pressure with 5. After the forcing sequence to 12, White captures five stones. (Black should not be satisfied with playing 5 at 6 and only picking off a few stones.)

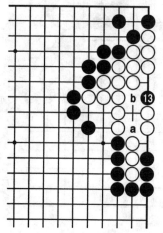

Continuation- Black plays back in at 13, making miai of 'a' and 'b'. White is dead.

Problem 39
White to play

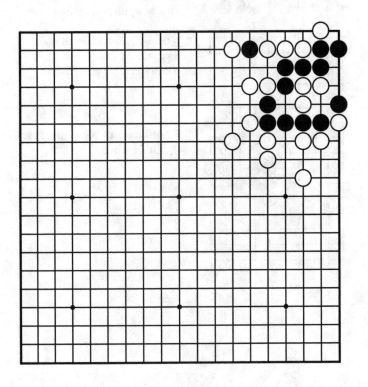

Can White kill the black
corner?

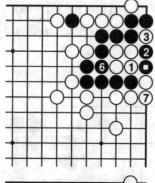

Correct Answer- The atari at white 1 is the vital move. Black sacrifices one more stone at 2, trying to confuse the opponent. With the moves through 7, Black captures six white stones.

4 throws in at the marked stone
5 captures at 2
8 captures at the marked stone

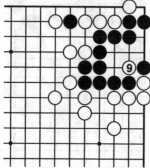

Continuation- White plays back in at 9, killing Black.

Problem 40
Black to play

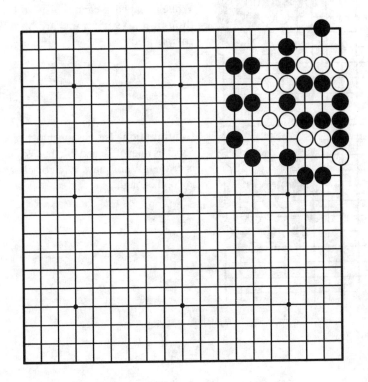

How can Black kill the
white group?

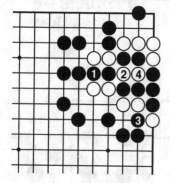

Correct Answer- Black connects at 1 and White naturally throws in at 2. Black 3 sacrifices 7 black stones. White captures with 4. (Black 3 at 4, giving White a snapback-capture also works, though the variations are more complicated.)

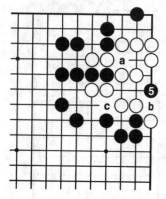

Continuation- The placement at black 5 makes miai of 'a' and 'b', thus White is dead. If White plays at 'c', black 'a' is good enough.

Problem 41
Black to play

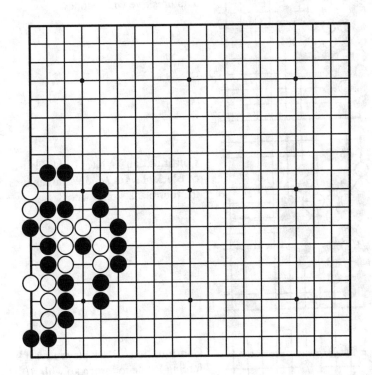

Can this white group be killed?

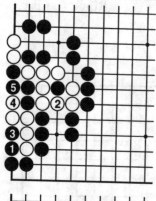

Correct Answer- The extension at black 1 is inevitable. Through 5, Black captures five white stones.

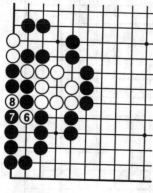

Continuation- White plays back in at 6. Black plays at 7 and White captures the four black stones with 8.

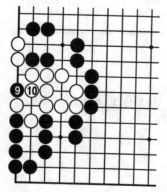

Continuation- Black plays atari at 9, forcing White to form a ko with 10.

Problem 42
Black to play

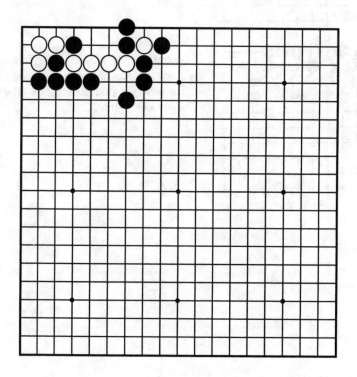

What's the status of the white group?

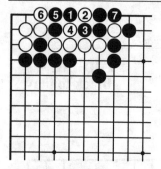

Correct Answer- Black plays a diagonal move at 1. White throws in at 2. Through 8, White captures three black stones. However, Black can recapture at 9, giving White a false eye.

8 captures at 2, 9 captures at 1

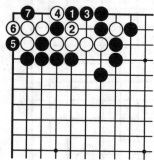

Variation- If white 2 is played here instead, Black happily connects at 3. Through the placement at 7, Black easily kills White.

Problem 43
White to play

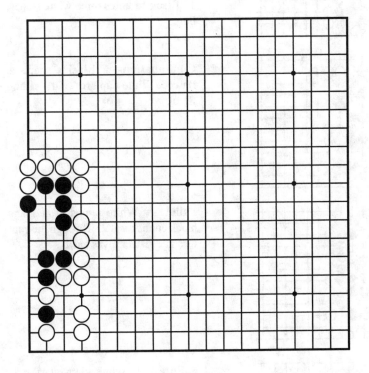

How can White kill the black group?

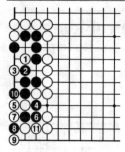

Correct Answer- The combination of 1 and 3 displays keen judgement. When Black then cuts off a stone with 4, White's descent to 5 is the perfect follow-up. Black connects at 6, and White feeds a stone with 7. With 8 to 12 Black captures three white stones, but...

12 at 8

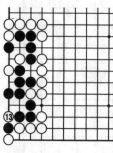

Continuation- ...Black's shape is flawed. White captures at 13 killing Black.

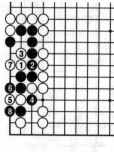

Failure- White jumps in at 1 and black connects at 2. Through the capture at 8, Black lives easily.

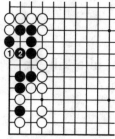

Failure- If White plays atari at 1, Black forms a ko at 2.

Problem 44
Black to play

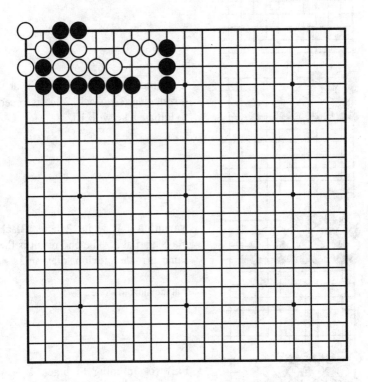

Is the white group alive or dead?

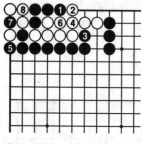

Correct Answer- Black's extension at 1, feeding one more stone, is the key. Through 8, White captures four black stones.

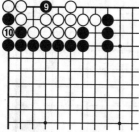

Continuation- Black plays in at 9 threatening a snapback. White is forced to initiate a ko with 10.

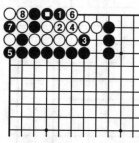

Variation- If white 2 here, Black plays atari at 3. The end result is the same as in the previous diagram.

9 at the marked stone

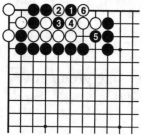

Failure- Jumping to black 1 is a mistake because White has the effective throw-in at 2. After the atari at 6 it is clear that White has made life cleanly.

Problem 45
White to play

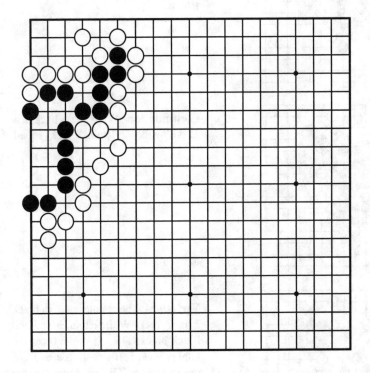

Black has neglected to reinforce this side group. How can White punish him?

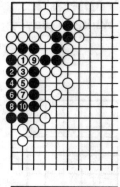

Answer- Black 2 in reply to the atari of white 1 is a mistake. White crimps down Black's eye space with the sacrifice up to 9, feeding five stones to Black.

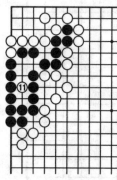

Continuation- White plays back in at 11 taking the vital point. Black is dead.

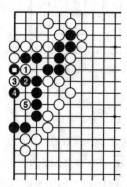

Variation- The counter-atari of black 2 is correct. White captures at 3 and Black blocks at 4. If White takes the vital point at 5, Black starts a ko at the marked stone. If White connects at the marked stone, Black makes unconditional life at 5.

Problem 46
Black to play

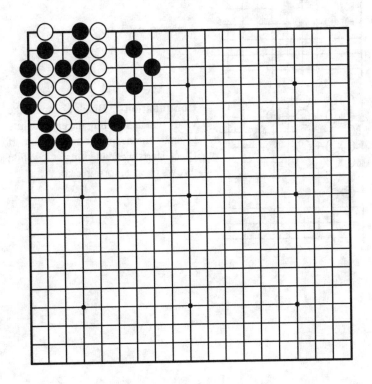

What's the best local result Black can get?

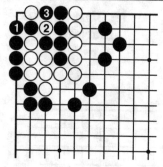

Correct Answer- Black connects at 1 and White throws in at 2. Black 3 looks clumsy, but is actually a good move. White captures six black stones with 4.

4 captures at 2

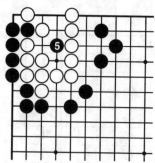

Continuation- Black occupies the vital point at 5, killing the entire white group. In the previous diagram, if Black starts by connecting at 2, White throws in at 1, forming ko.

Problem 47
Black to play

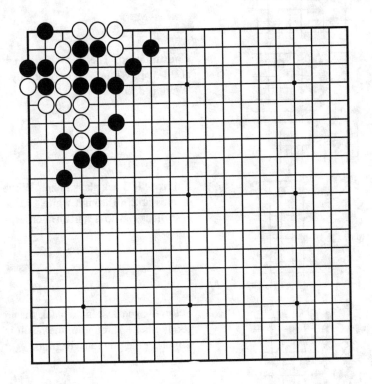

How can Black win this
fight?

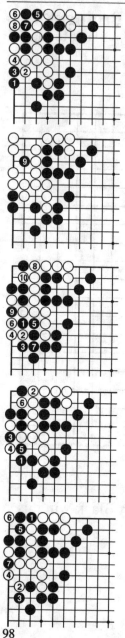

Correct Answer- The 'bungee jump' of black 1 is a far-sighted, calculated move. Through 8, White captures six black stones.

Continuation- The black placement at 9 leaves White with only one eye. White is dead.

Failure- If Black plays 1 here, White clamps at 2. Through white 10, the best Black can do is start an approach-move ko.

Failure- The descent to black 1 is no good either. Through 6, the result is similar to the previous diagram.

Failure- Black 1 here is premature. White replies by clamping at 2. Through the atari at white 6, Black's position is hopeless. Black captures at 7 trying to form a ko. But Black is just wasting moves, as it is only an approach-move ko.

Problem 48
Black to play

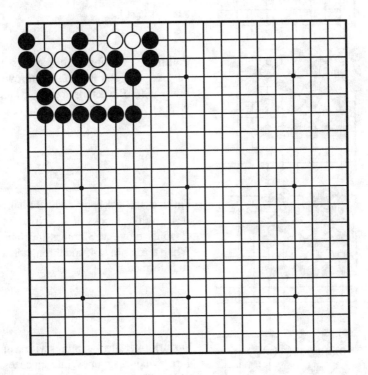

Can Black kill the white corner?

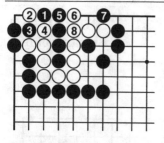

Correct Answer- The diagonal play at 1 is brilliant. White jumps down to 2 and Black thrusts in at 3. Up to the throw-in at 9, the white corner is killed.

9 throws in at 1

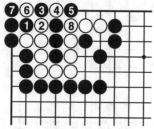

Failure- Turning at black 1 is a mistake. White thrusts at 2, then throws in at 4 and 6. Black fails to connect and White lives.

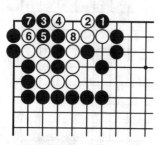

Failure- If Black begins with the hane at 1, White blocks at 2. Now the diagonal move at 3 comes too late. White throws in at 4, and through 8, a ko is formed.

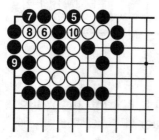

Variation- If Black captures with 5 in the previous diagram, White squeezes with 6. Through the atari at 10, **Black** fails to connect and White lives.

Problem 49
Black to play

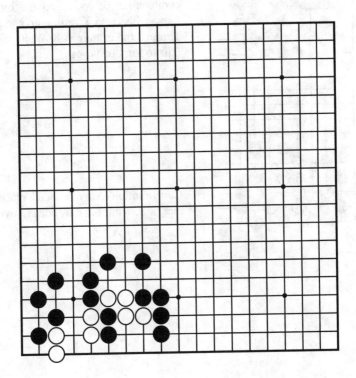

Is the white group alive?

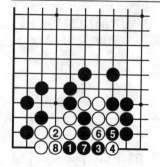

Correct Answer- Black plays a combination of hane and diagonal move with 1 and 3, setting up a trap. Through the capture at 8, White still fails to form two eyes.

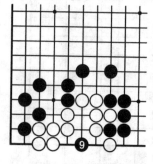

Continuation- After the black placement at 9, White has only one real eye.

Problem 50
White to play

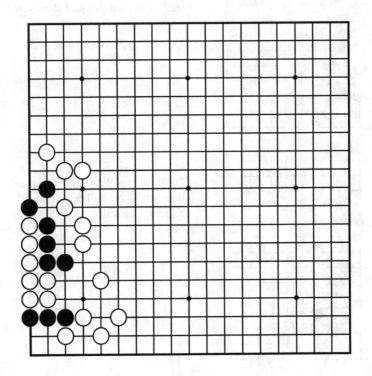

Can White capture the black group?

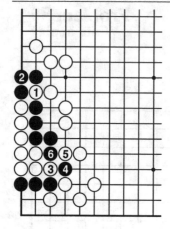

Correct Answer- White plays atari at 1 and extends at 3. When Black blocks at 4, White clamps the stone with 5. Black captures a block of stones with 6.

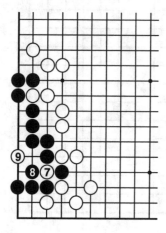

Continuation- White throws in at 7 prompting black 8. The placement at white 9 then kills the entire black group.

Problem 51
Black to play

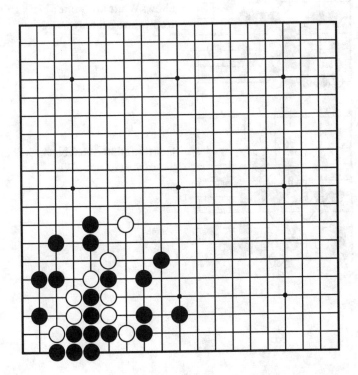

It's a turmoil in the corner.
What's the most aggres-
sive way for Black to
play?

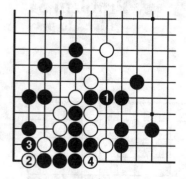

Correct Answer- The connection at black 1 is an inspired move. This allows White to capture a black group from white 2 through 4.....

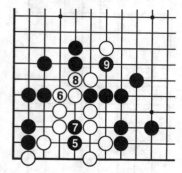

Continuation- ...but black 5, 7 and 9 turn the tables on White.

Problem 52
Black to play

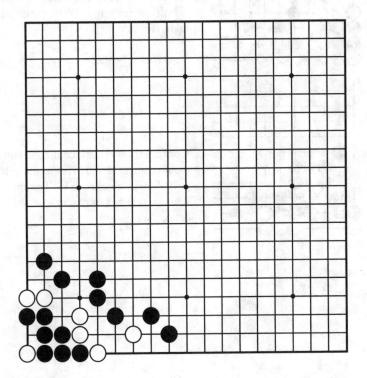

It looks like the black group in the corner is surrounded and will die. Can Black kill the white group instead?

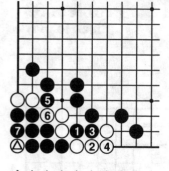

Correct Answer- The atari at black 1 is brilliant, leading to White capturing eight stones with 8 .

8 captures at the marked stone.

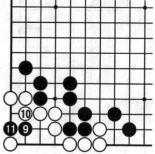

Continuation- Black continues with the placement at 9. If White connects at 10, Black descends to 11. The entire white group has only one eye and is dead.

Problem 53
White to play

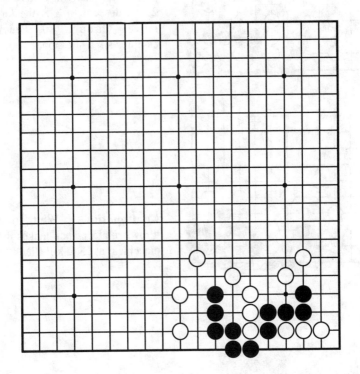

What will be the result of
the capturing race in the
corner?

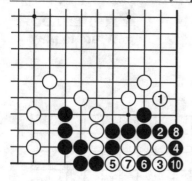

Correct Answer- White calmly plays at 1. When Black blocks at 2, the descent to 3 is the key move. Through 10, Black captures six white stones.

9 connects at 6

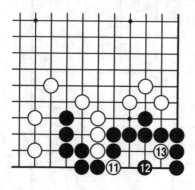

Continuation- White first throws in at 11, then makes the placement at 13 to kill Black.

Problem 54
White to play

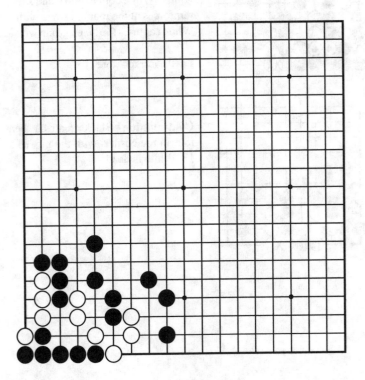

Which side will win the
battle in the corner?

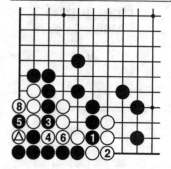

Correct Answer- Black cuts at 1 prompting White to connect at 2. Black cuts again with 3 and then captures with 5. White connects at 6 and Black reinforces at the marked stone with 7. White captures the black group with 8.

7 at the marked stone

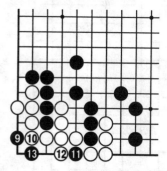

Continuation- Black creates a 'bent four in the corner' with the moves to 13. White is dead.

Problem 55
White to play

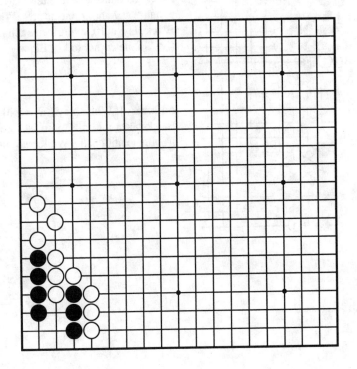

What will be the result of the fight in the corner? Can White kill Black?

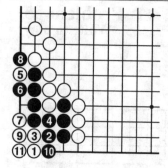

Correct Answer- The placement at white 1 is splendid, forcing Black to turn at 2. White extends to 3, prompting Black to connect. White throws-in at 5, hanes at 7 and connects at 9. When Black plays at 10, White forms a 'bulky five' in the corner to kill Black.

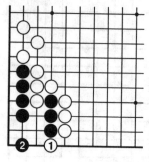

Failure- If White plays hane with 1, Black takes the vital point at 2, and lives unconditionally. White has failed.

Problem 56
Black to play

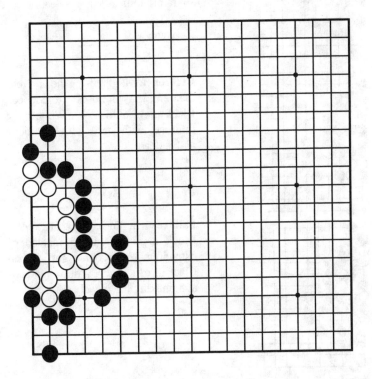

Can Black kill the white group?

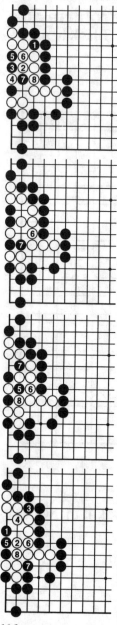

Correct Answer- Black pressures White with 1 and threatens a snapback with 3. Through 6, White captures two black stones. Black then gives atari at 7 and captures at 9, forming a 'pyramid four'. White is dead.

9 captures at 3

Reference Diagram- In the previous diagram, if White uses 6 to connect, Black plays atari at 7. White can't reinforce both ataris with one move and is dead.

Failure- In the correct answer, if Black captures with 5 instead of extending, White connects at 6. When Black throws in at 7, White plays atari at 8, making life cleanly.

Failure- The order of moves is crucial. If Black plays 1 directly, White achieves seki with the moves to 8.

Problem 57
Black to play

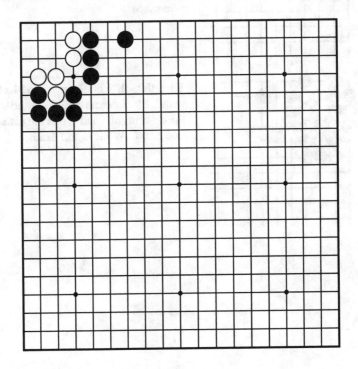

How can Black kill the white corner? Finding the first move is easy, but try to read out the continuation.

117

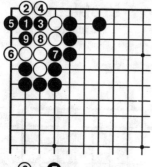

Correct Answer- The placement at 1 strikes the vital point in this shape. White attaches underneath and Black extends to 3. Through 9, Black reduces White's eye space to the dead bulky-five shape.

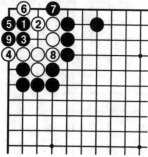

Variation- If White bumps into Black with 2, Black extends to 3, followed by the descents of 4 and 5, and the hanes of 6 and 7. White is still dead.

Problem 58
White to play

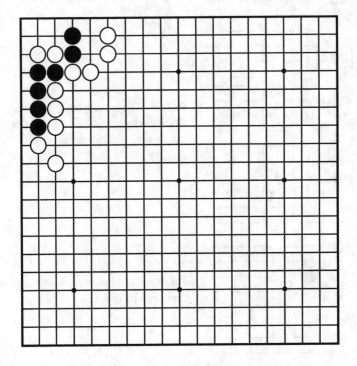

Find the right move to
win the capturing race in
the corner.

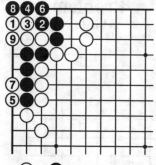

Correct Answer- White makes an exquisite diagonal move with 1. Black turns at 2 and White blocks at 3. Through 9, White reduces Black's eye-space to a bulky-five, killing Black.

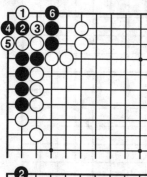

Failure- The jump to white 1 is clumsy. Black wedges in at 2, and makes life in the corner with moves through 6.

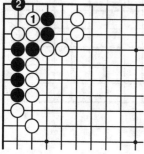

Failure- Turning with white 1 here is answered by black 2.

Problem 59
Black to play

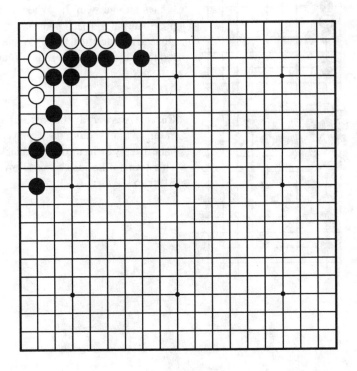

Can Black pull anything
off in the corner?

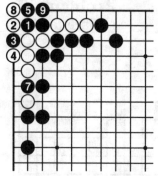

White Resists- The extension to 1 is the key. When White hanes at 2, Black plays the brilliant throw-in at 3. If White captures, Black descends to 5. White connect at 3 with 6, and Black breaks an eye with 7. When White plays atari at 8, Black adds one more stone to the sacrifice, killing White by reducing the shape to a square-four.

6 at 3

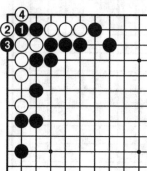

Correct Answer- In the previous diagram, White should have played a hane in reply to the throw-in at black 3. This forms a ko instead of allowing Black to kill cleanly.

Problem 60
White to play

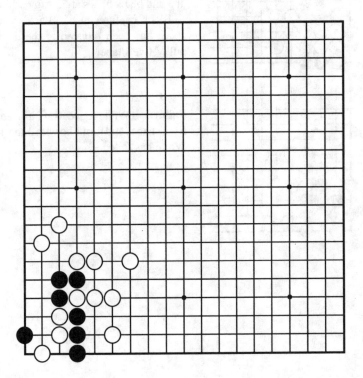

What will be the outcome
of the capturing race in
the corner?

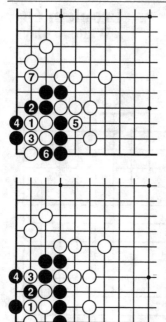

Correct Answer- White turns at 1 and Black blocks at 2. White connects at 3 and black hanes at 5. After white 5, Black captures at 6. Black's eye space has been reduced to the dead bulky-five shape.

Failure- If White connects at 1 instead, Black hanes and forms ko with 2 and 4. White has failed.

124

Problem 61
White to play

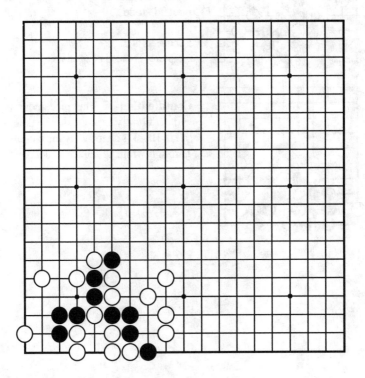

Can White capture the black group?

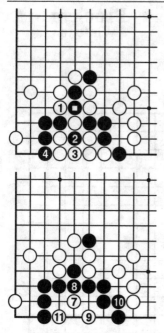

Correct Answer- White captures first at 1 and again at 3, after Black's throw-in at 2. Black plays atari at 4 and White connects at 2 with 5. Black captures eight white stone by playing 6 at the marked stone.

5 connects at 2
6 captures at the marked stone

Continuation- The placement at white 7 bluntly exploits the weakness left in Black's shape after the capture. Through white 11, Black is dead.

Problem 62
Black to play

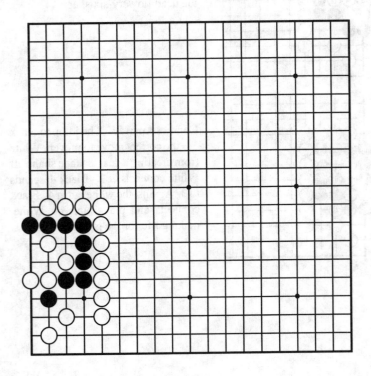

How should Black play
in order to win this fight?

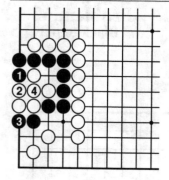

Failure- Turning at black 1 looks natural but is a mistake. White has no trouble reducing Black's eye space to the dead flowery-six shape.

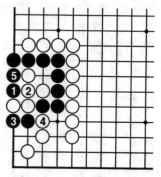

Correct Answer- The jump to black 1 is the correct move to prevent White from creating a dead nakade shape. If White connects at 2, Black descends to 3. Against the white cut at 4, Black connects and plays atari on White, making life for the group.

Problem 63
Black to play

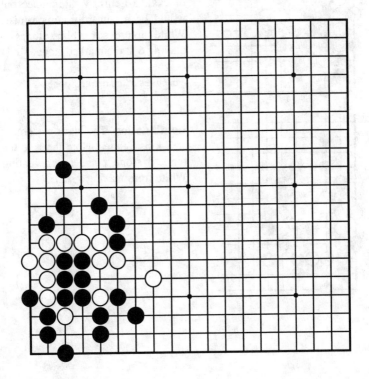

How should Black make
use of the ugly rectang-
ular six-stone clump?

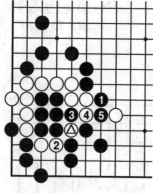

Correct Answer- Black hanes at 1, sealing in White. White plays atari at 2. Black captures a white stone with 3. When White plays atari at 4, Black blocks at 5. Letting White connect out would be a cowardly compromise. White captures seven black stones by playing 6 at the marked stone.

6 captures at the marked stone

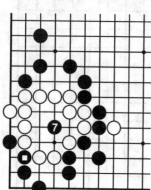

Continuation- The black placement at 7 kills White. Note the role the marked stone plays in preventing White from making a seki.

Problem 64
White to play

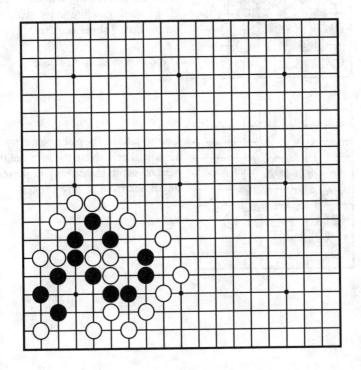

Can White capture the black group?

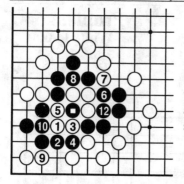

Correct Answer- The placement at white 1 is marvelous. White connects at the marked white stone with 11, setting up a 7 stone sacrifice.

11 connects at the marked stone

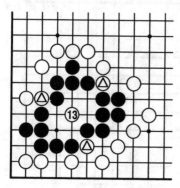

Continuation- The placement of white 13 kills Black. Note the role that the marked white stones play in preventing Black from getting a seki.

Problem 65
White to play

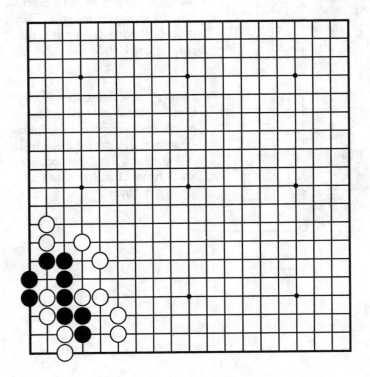

What will be the outcome of the capturing race in the corner?

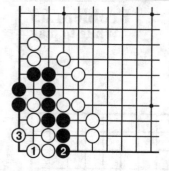

Correct Answer- White's turn at 1 is clever. Black must block at 2 and White makes a hanging connection with 3. Although Black can capture the white stones in the corner, a flowery-six shape is formed, and Black is dead. If White plays 1 at 3, Black plays at 1 and lives.

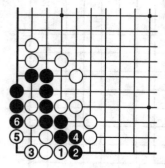

Failure- If White exchanges 1 for 2 here first, Black still manages to capture the white group, but capturing one extra stone forms a live shape for Black. If White plays 3 at 4, connecting out his 3 stones, Black cuts one space above 3 and lives.

Chapter 3
Other techniques

Problem 66
Black to play

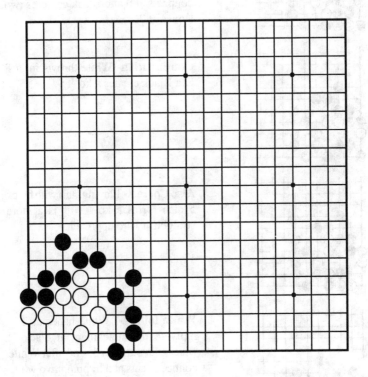

What's the best result
Black can get?

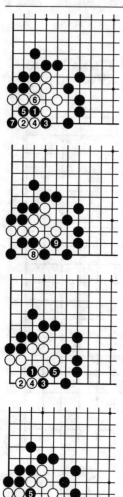

Correct Answer- Black gets a ko with the attachment at 1. White jumps to 2 and Black hanes at 3. When White extends to 4, one correct response is for Black to press along with 5. White connects at 6 and Black captures two stones at 7.

Continuation- White throws in at 8 and Black creates a ko at 9.

Also Correct- Playing atari with black 5 also forms a ko. This is a more straightforward approach.

White failure- White hanes at 2 in reply to the attachment at black 1. Black plays atari at 3, and after White connects, cuts at 5 trapping two white stones in a shortage of liberties. The white group is unconditionally dead.

Problem 67
Black to play

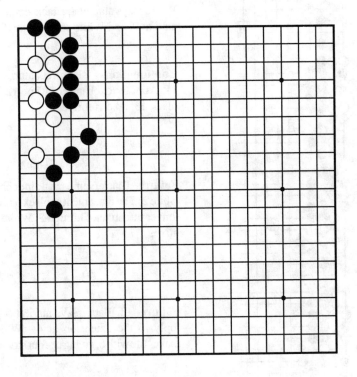

What's the best way to attack the white group in the corner?

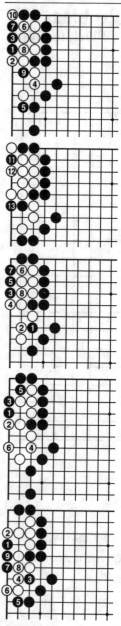

Correct Answer- Black 1 is the vital point. White descends to 2 and Black draws back at 3. This is followed by the extension of white 4, and the block at 5. After white 6, Black extends at 7. White plays atari at 8, Black counter-atari at 9, and White captures at 10.

Continuation- Black recaptures at 11. After the exchange of white 12 for black 13, a ko is formed.

Failure Black clamps at 1, inducing white 2. The placement at black 3 is no longer effective. Through 8, White is alive.

Failure- If Black plays atari at 5 in reply to the extension at 4, White makes life with 6, giving up four stones.

Variation- Blocking at 2 in reply to black 1 is a mistake. White dies with the moves to black 9.

Problem 68
White to play

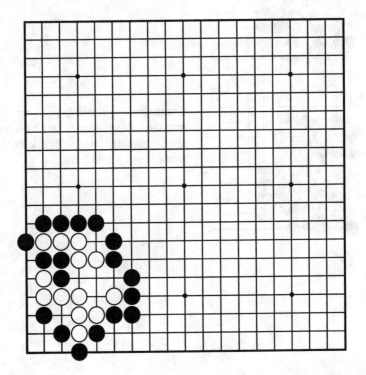

Can White live in the corner?

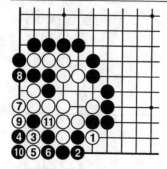

Correct Answer- White first cuts at 1 in sente, then cuts at 3 and descends to 5. The sequence is exquisite. After White plays atari at 11...

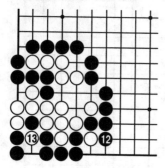

Continuation- ...Black is forced to grip the cutting stone with 12. After White captures at 13, Black can't connect and White lives.

Problem 69
White to play

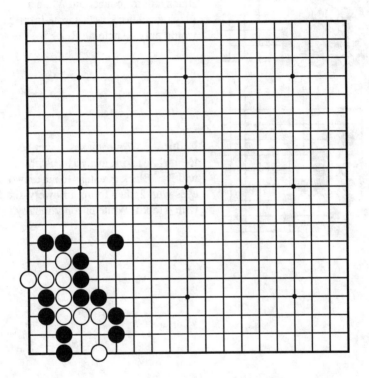

White is to make life. Be careful—Black may have a trick up his sleeve.

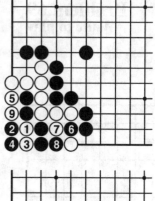

Correct Answer- The cut at white 1 is brilliant. Through the atari at white 9, Black fails to connect and White lives. Playing white 5 as a throw-in at 1 would only be helping Black.

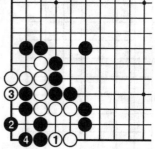

Failure- White makes a bamboo-joint while taking away a black liberty with 1. Black threatens to make two eyes with 2, then forms a flowery-six with 4 to kill White unconditionally.

Problem 70
White to play

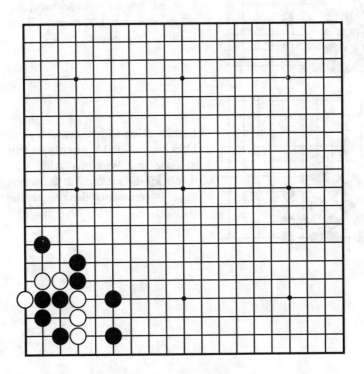

Who will win the skirmish in the corner?

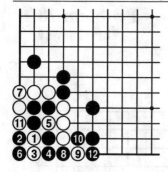

Correct Answer- Playing in at 1 is splendid. When Black plays atari at 2, White descends to 3. Through 12, Black captures three stones.

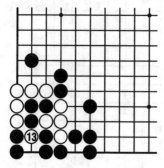

Continuation- White captures three black stones with 13. Since black fails to connect out, White makes life. Note that Black did not use 7 to throw in at 1, as is commonly done in similar positions.

Problem 71
Black to play

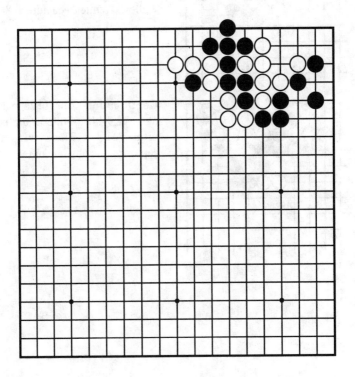

Win the capturing race
unconditionally.

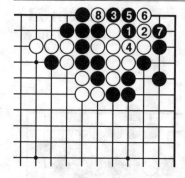

Correct Answer- Black 1 is at the vital point. Black links up underneath with 3 and connects at 5. Playing 5 at 6 would give ko. When White plays atari at 6, black 7 allows White to capture at 8.

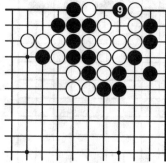

Continuation- The black placement at 9 hits White at the new vital point. Black wins the capturing race by one move.

Problem 72
Black to play

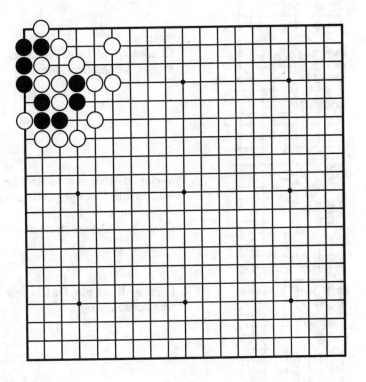

How can Black make life
in the corner?

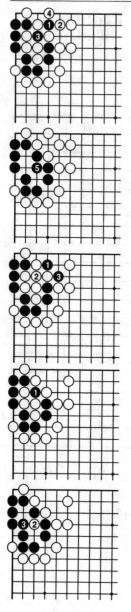

Correct Answer- Black 1 buys the time he needs to live. White plays atari at 2, and Black's capture at 3 forces white 4.

Continuation- Black reinforces at 5, making unconditional life.

Variation- The connection at 2 here is not playable. Black plays atari at 3 and White suffers a territorial loss compared with the correct answer.

Failure- Black plays here, capturing the stones right off...

Continuation- White plays atari at 2. Black is forced into a ko.

Problem 73
Black to play

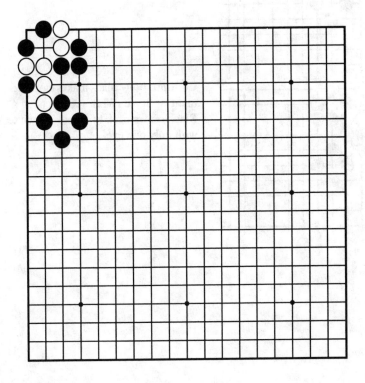

Perhaps white has played
too optimistically here.

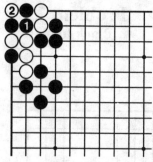

Correct Answer- Black 1 is clever, forcing White to capture at 2.

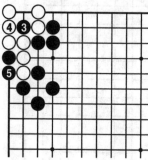

Continuation- Black makes the placement at 3. If White connects at 4, Black draws back to 5, leaving white with only one eye.

Problem 74
Black to play

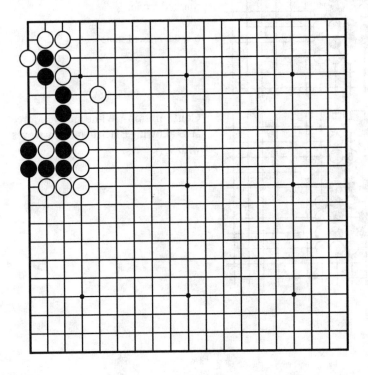

Is the black group on the side alive?

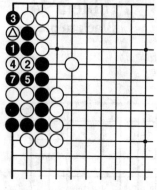

Correct Answer- Black turns at 1 tempting White to play atari at 2. When black captures at 3, White plays atari at 4. Black's atari at 5 forces White to capture three black stones with 6 at the marked stone.

6 at the marked stone

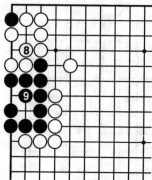

Continuation- White must reinforce at 8, allowing Black to make two eyes with 9.

152

Problem 75
Black to play

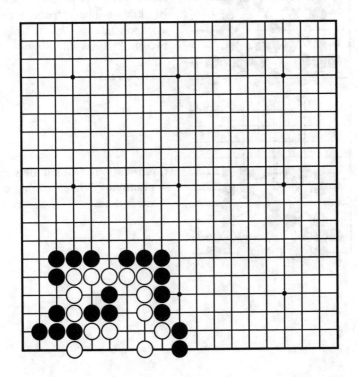

Is the white group alive?

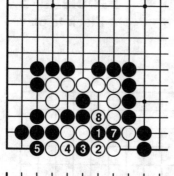

Correct Answer- Black plays hane at 1, then throws in at 3 and plays atari at 5 to reduce white's eye space. Black then brilliantly feeds one more stone to white at 7. White captures two black stones with 8.

6 connects at 3

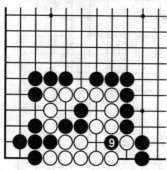

Continuation- Black throws in at 9, destroying White's second eye. White is dead.

Problem 76
White to play

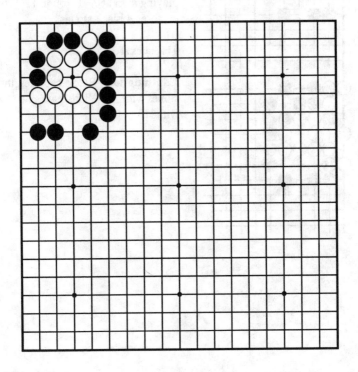

Can White make life in
the corner?

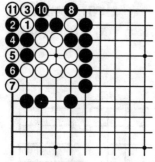

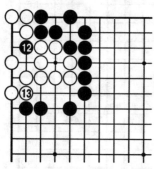

Correct Answer- The cut at white 1 is the key. Black plays atari at 2 and connects at 4, trying to form an under-the-stones shape. However, White manages by throwing in at 5 and playing atari at 7. Through 11, White captures 4 black stones.

9 captures at 5

Continuation- Black captures three stones with 12. White makes two eyes with 13.

156

Problem 77
Black to play

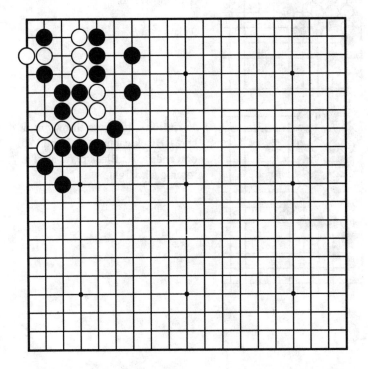

How should black play the capturing race?

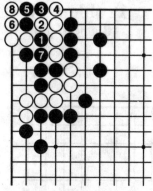

Answer- The wedge at black 1 is exquisite, forcing White to play atari from the top with 2. When Black hanes at 3, White descends to 4. After the moves to 8, Black plays back in at 5 killing White.

9 plays in at 5

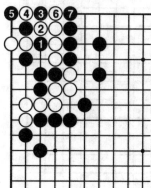

Variation- If White throws in at 4 here, Black captures at 5 and White descends to 6. Black plays atari at 7, forcing a ko fight.

Problem 78
Black to play

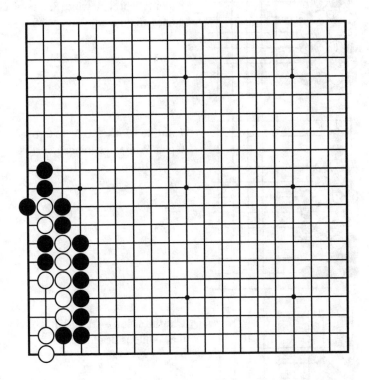

Can the white group in the corner survive Black's attack?

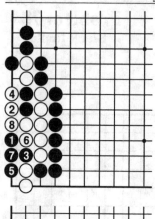

Correct Answer- The placement at black 1 is correct. White plays atari at 2, and Black cuts at 3. This is a powerful move, allowing White to capture. Through white 8, four black stones are in atari, but...

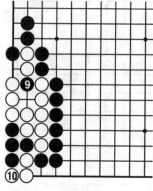

Continuation- ...Black's throw-in at 9 puts White in a tough spot.

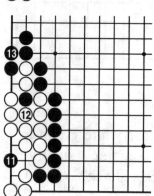

Continuation- After 13, it is obvious that White is dead.

Problem 79
White to play

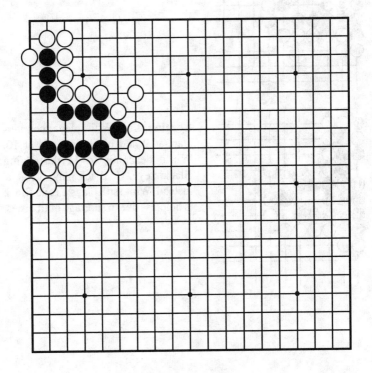

Can White kill the large
black group?

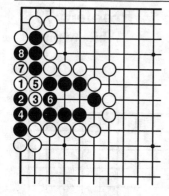

Correct Answer- White 1 is the vital point. Through 7, an under-the-stones shape is formed. Black captures four white stones with 8.

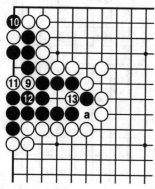

Continuation- White plays a counter-atari at 9 and black captures at 10. White descends to 11 destroying Black's eye. If Black plays 12 at 'a' instead, White still plays 13 and Black is helpless due to shortage of liberties.

Problem 80
Black to play

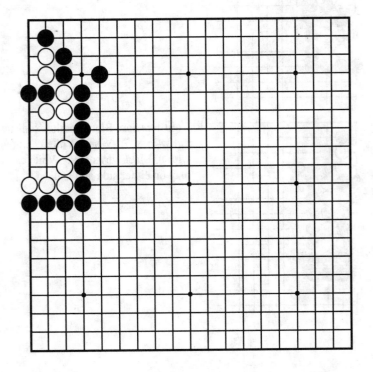

Is the white group on the side alive?

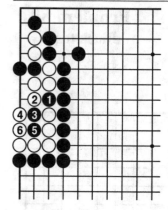

Correct Answer- Black pushes in and cuts with 1 and 3, then makes the clever extension to 5. White captures two black stones with 6.

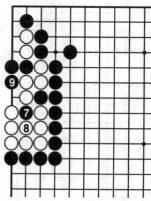

Continuation- Black has the exquisite throw-in at 7. When White captures with 8, Black turns at 9. White can't play on either side and is dead.

Problem 81
Black to play

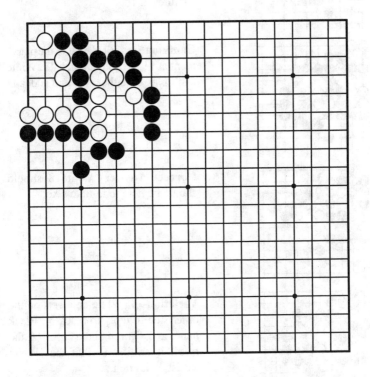

Is the white corner group alive?

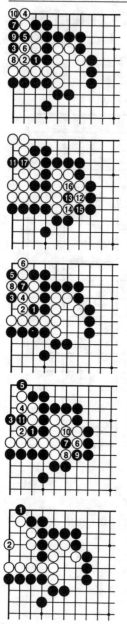

White Resists- The thrust at black 1 is the correct answer, followed by the placement at 3. When Black hanes at 7, white 8 is a mistake, allowing Black to form a pyramid-four shape. White captures at 10.

Continuation- Black makes the placement at 11. Through black 17, White can't play on either side and is dead.

Correct Answer- White 8 should should be here to initiate a ko.

Variation- If White connects on the other side in reply to black 3. Black hanes at 5. Through the cut at 11, the result is similar to that the 'White Resists' diagram.

Failure- Black plays a hane with 1 instead. White jumps to 2 and is alive. Black has failed.

Problem 82
Black to play

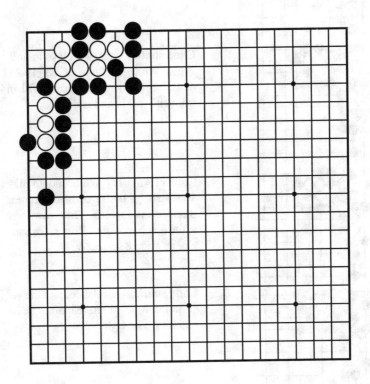

Can Black kill the white corner?

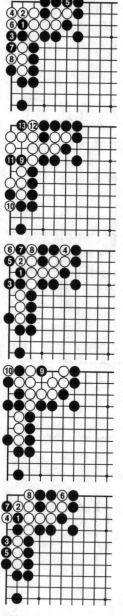

White Resists- The combination of 1 and 3 is the correct answer, aiming at forming an under-the-stones shape. White 4 is a mistake. Through 8, White captures four black stones, but...

Continuation- ...Black plays in at 9. When White captures at 10, Black descends to 11. White can't fill in from either side and is dead.

Correct Answer- White should play 4 as atari on the three black stones. Black forms a ko at 5. The throw-in at white 6 is important. Both sides capture at 7 and 8 respectively.

Continuation- Black occupies the vital point at 9. White captures at 10 initiating a ko fight.

Failure- Black uses 3 to play atari on the three white stones. This crude move allows White to live easily.

Problem 83
White to play

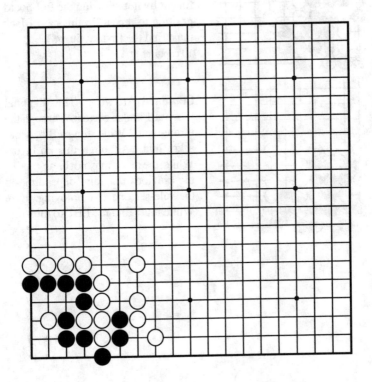

It is not too hard to make a ko here. But can you sniff out any peculiarity in the position?

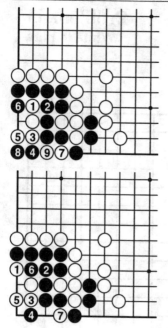

Bizarre Variation- White extends to 1 and Black connects at 2. Through the recapture at 10, an "eternal-life" ko is created. (Note: According to the Super-Ko rule, the "eternal life" ko is fought by not allowing the full-board position to repeat. In this case Black must find the first ko threat.)

10 captures at 4

Standard Answer- The diagonal move at 1 is also correct. Through the throw-in at 7 White forces Black into a ko fight. Although this ko favors White, the result may not be as good as the previous diagram, depending on the rule-set one is employing. Here White must find the first ko threat.

Problem 84
White to play

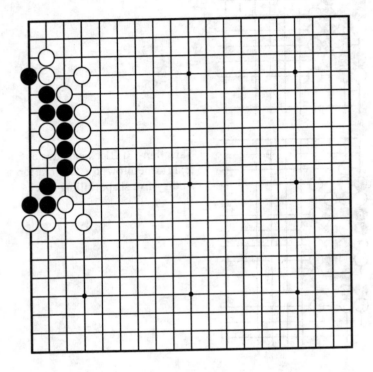

Is the black group on the
side alive?

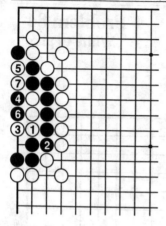

Correct Answer- White extends 1, descends to 3 and throws-in at 5, aiming to kill Black unconditionally. The feeding of a stone at black 6 is exquisite. An "eternal-life" ko is the result.

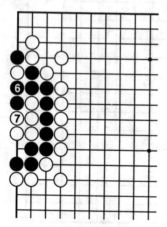

Variation- If Black captures at 6 in reply to the throw-in at 5. White forms a bulky-five shape killing Black.

Problem 85
White to play

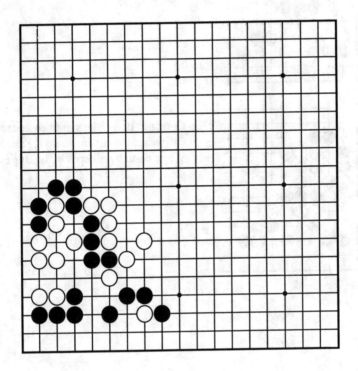

Can White rescue his surrounded group?

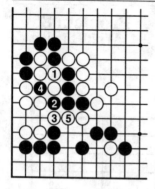

Correct Answer- White connects at 1, allowing Black to play atari at 2. This is a very clever play. Through white 5, Black captures four white stones.

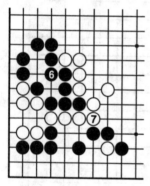

Continuation- Black must connect at 6 to prevent White from playing there. White casually escapes by linking up at 7.

Problem 86
White to play

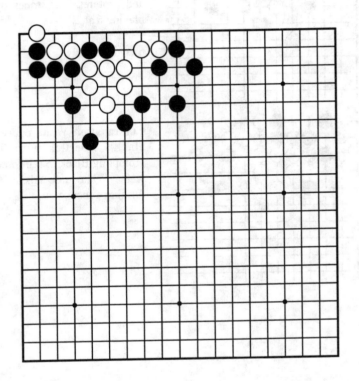

Can White make life on
the upper side?

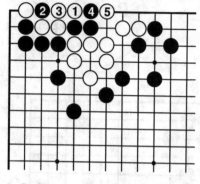

Correct Answer- The hane at white 1 is brilliant. Black throws-in at 2, plays atari at 4 and captures four stones by playing 6 at 2.

6 captures at 2

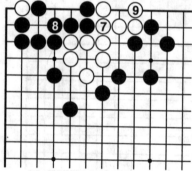

Continuation- White reduces black's liberties with 7, prompting Black to reinforce at 8. White descends to 9 forming a second eye.

Problem 87
Black to play

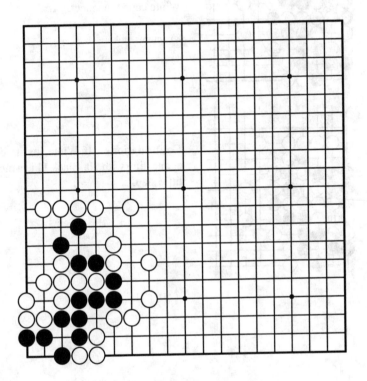

Can Black make life for
the corner group?

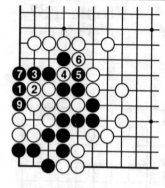

Correct Answer- Jumping down to black 1 is the key. When Black plays atari on the three white stones with 9, White cannot connect.

8 captures at 4

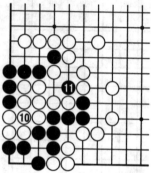

Continuation- If White insists on connecting with 10, black 11 is a nice little slap.

Problem 88
White to play

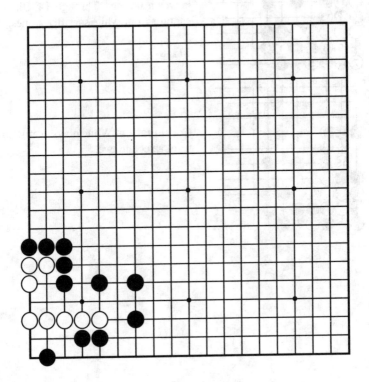

Can White make life in
the corner?

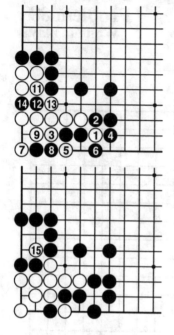

Correct Answer- White makes an eye in sente with the sequence to 10. The attachment at white 7 in particular is worth noting. Through 14, Black captures four white sacrifice stones.

10 at 8

Continuation- White plays in at 15 to form a second eye.

Problem 89
Black to play

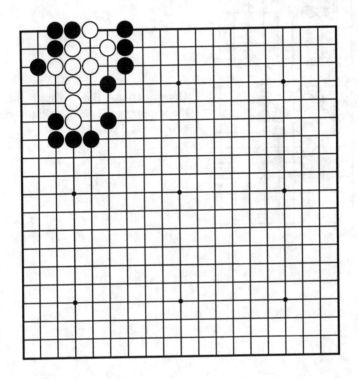

How can Black kill White?

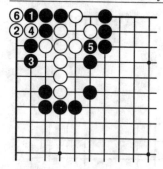

Correct Answer- Turning at black 1 is exquisite. White makes the placement of 2 and Black draws back to 3. Through 6, White captures six black stones.

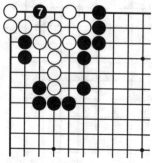

Continuation- Black plays in with the placement at 7. White fails to form two eyes and is dead.

Problem 90
White to play

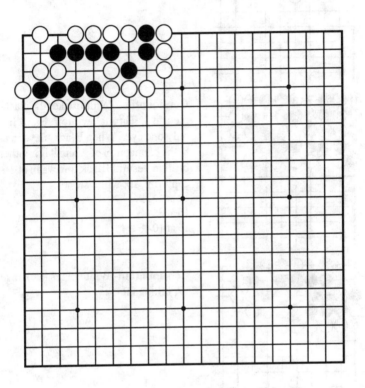

Can White kill the black group?

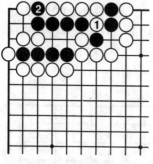

Correct Answer- Feeding an extra stone at white 1 is very far-sighted. Black captures at 2.

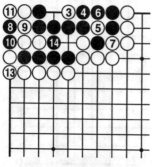

Continuation- White makes the placement at 3. Through white 7, Black has only one eye. When Black plays in at 8, the connection of white 9 is another brilliant tesuji. Black throws in at 16, capturing six white stones.

12 at 10
15 at 8
16 at 10

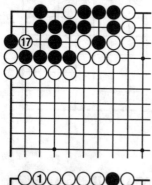

Continuation- White plays back in at 17, killing Black.

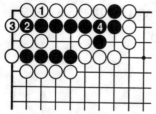

Failure- The connection at white 1 is a mistake. Black thrusts at 2 and plays atari at 4, making life easily. White at most captures four black stones.

Problem 91
White to play

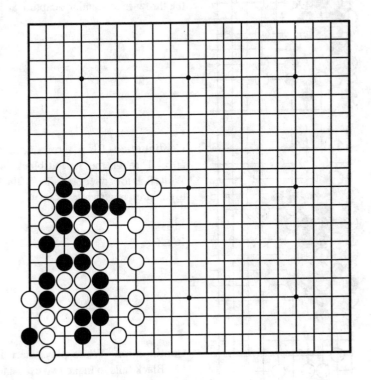

Which side will win the
capturing race?

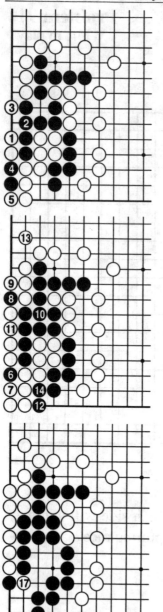

Correct Answer- The atari at white 1 is the only move. This is followed by the connection at black 2, the hane at 3, the throw-in at 4 and the capture at 5.

Continuation- Black throws back in at 6. Through the atari at black 14, White fails to connect and allows Black to capture a large white group with 16.

15 at 8
16 at 6

Continuation- White plays atari at 17. Black fails to make two eyes and is dead.

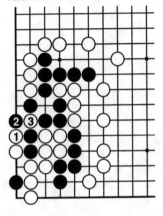

Variation Diagram-When White plays atari at 1, Black makes a hanging connection at 2, giving up two stones for one.

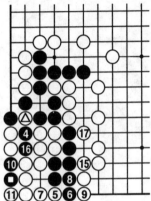

Continuation- Black recaptures at 4, trying to kill White in the capturing race. White attaches underneath with 5. Through white 17, Black loses the capturing race by one move.

12 at 10
13 at the marked black stone
14 at the marked white stone

Index and Glossary

diagonal move *a diagonal extension from a stone* 22, 36, 48, 52, 68, 88, 100, 102, 120, 170

E

'eternal-life' ko   *a repetitive position which is ko under the super-ko rule, and can lead to a game being annulled under Japanese rules* 170, 172

F

flowery-six *a kind of oversized eye(nakade)* 3, 128, 134, 142

H

hane *a diagonal move played in contact with the enemy (bending around an enemy stone)* 16, 22, 26, 36, 48, 54, 68, 72, 76, 78, 100, 102, 114, 122, 124, 130, 136, 154, 166, 176, 186

hanging connection *playing adjacent to a cutting point to protect it* 22, 48, 134, 187

K

ko *a repetitive situation in which one may not immediately recapture* 3, 8, 22, 24, 26, 28, 32, 40, 46, 48, 52, 54, 56, 60, 62, 64, 66, 68, 70, 72, 76, 86, 90, 92, 94, 96, 100, 122, 124, 136, 138, 146, 148, 158, 166, 168, 169

ko threat *a move played elsewhere to gain the right to retake a ko* 61, 170

M

miai *two points related such that if I take one, you take the other and vice versa* 8, 48, 80, 84

O

oversized eye(nakade) *a large eye-space typically having a single vital point for dividing it into two eyes* 3, 8, 128

P

peep *a move played adjacent to a cutting point threatening to extend in* 52

placement *an attacking move typically played inside an opposing group, but not in contact with any enemy stones* 8, 17, 20, 22, 30, 40, 42, 44, 48, 58, 62, 72, 74, 78, 84, 88, 98, 102, 104, 108, 110, 114, 118, 126, 130, 132, 138, 150, 160, 166, 182, 184

pyramid-four *an oversized eye(nakade) shape* 3, 116, 166

S

seki *a way of living by bringing about an impasse in which neither group in a capturing race can put the other in atari without exposing itself to capture* 14, 28, 50, 116, 130, 132

sente *the initiative, a move requiring an answer* 140, 180

shortage of liberties *a position in which one cannot play on a certain important point without putting oneself in atari* 3, 46, 58, 136, 162

snapback *an immediate recapture based on shortage of liberties* 40, 42, 54, 66, 84, 92, 116

square-four *an oversized eye(nakade) shape differing from the others in that there is no way to make two eyes of it with a single move* 122

T

tesuji *a clever move exploiting the special charac-
teristics of a local situation* 18, 36, 40, 44, 184

throw-in *a single stone played deliberately into
atari* 3, 6, 10, 18, 40, 52, 54, 56, 60, 64, 70, 72,
74, 76, 82, 84, 88, 92, 96, 100, 104, 110, 114,
122, 126, 142, 144, 154, 156, 158, 164, 168,
170, 172, 186

U

under-the-stones *a dramatic recapture where one
plays into the space vacated by sacrifice
stones* 3, 8, 11 14, 15, 16, 17, 28, 29, 30, 32,
44, 46, 48, 49, 52, 62, 156, 162, 168

V

vital point *the key point in a position that must be
occupied* 3, 16, 20, 22, 70, 76, 94, 96, 114,
118, 138, 146, 162, 168

W

wedge *a move played in between two enemy stones
such that one is clamped* 6, 120, 158

Other Books From Yutopian

Sakata Series
Killer of Go
Tesuji and Anti-Suji of Go

The Nihon Ki-In Series
A Compendium of Trick Plays
100 Challenging Go Problems for 100 Days of Study
Pro-Pro Handicap Go

Go Handbook Series
Proverbs
Fuseki   (available 1999)

Chinese Professional Series
Nie WeiPing on Go
Thirty-Six Stratagems Applied to Go, by Ma XiaoChun
Beauty and the Beast, Exquisite Play and Go Theory by Shen Guosun
Golden Opportunities by Rin Kaiho
Winning A Won Game, by Go Seigen
Yang Yilun's Ingenious Life and Death Puzzles, vol. 1 and 2
Essential Joseki by Rui Naiwei
Power Builder, vol. 1, by Wang Runan
Power Builder, vol 2, by Wang Runan   (available 1999)
Strategic Fundamentals in Go, by Guo Tisheng

Art of Go Series
Art of Connecting Stones
Art of Capturing

Pocket Book Series, by Yang Yilun
Rescue and Capture
Tricks in Joseki   (available 1999)

Korean Professional Series
Cho HunHyun's Go Techniques, vol. 1
Lee ChangHo's Novel Plays and Shapes   (available 1999)

Other Books From Yutopian
Fighting Ko
Utilizing Outward Influence
Master Go in Ten Days
Dramatic Moments on the Go Board
Igo Hatsuyo-ron, vol. 1

Book Descriptions

The Art of Connecting Stones by Wu Piao and Yu Xing
The Art of Connecting Stones is a problem book covering connections: along the edge of the board, made by capturing stones, using influence of friendly forces, and in the endgame.

Beauty and the Beast, Exquisite Play and Go Theory by Shen Guosun
The author gives us biographical information, anecdotes, and playing-style profiles on the leading 1980's Chinese players. Some of this material is not available in any other form, because it stems from the author's intimate knowledge of the players as his colleagues and friends.

A Compendium of Trick Plays by The Nihon Kiin
Tricks, traps, pitfalls and pratfalls, ruses and subterfuge, hocus pocus, snares and ambushes. With almost 900 diagrams in 220 pages, this is one of the great bargains on the market!

Cho Hun-Hyeon's Lectures on Go Techniques
Provides the basic fundamentals of Go. Basic shapes are analyzed covering Surrounding, Escaping, Connecting, Cutting, Attachments, Diagonals, Tigers (Hangs), Empty Triangles, and Hanes as well as basic techniques for Attachments, Extensions, Establishing A Base, Running Towards Center, Capping, Ataris, Cuts, Tigers, and Weaknesses.

Dramatic Moments on the Go Board by Abe Yoshiteru
Fascinating behind-the-scenes stories of unique and unusual occurrences in professional Go. Blunders and mis-readings by top players such as Go Seigen, Sakata Eio and Fujisawa Shuko are presented by Abe 9 Dan, a born raconteur. 220 pages with glossary and indices.

Essential Joseki, from The Masters of Go Series by Rui Naiwei 9 dan.
A handy joseki reference. The author provides advice on when to choose each variation based on the whole-board situation. Potential ladders, ko fights, and seki are explained to understand the conditions when a particular joseki can or cannot be played.

Fighting Ko by Jin Jiang
This book catalogues the wide variety of ko situations that one is likely to encounter over the board, as well as several that may not appear in the course of a lifetime of playing. Mastering the subject matter presented in this book will add potent weapons to any player's game.

Golden Opportunities by Rin Kaiho
Game positions are explained through compelling analogies with historical events in a way that repays re-reading the book many times. New insights will be found each time.

Killer of Go by Eio Sakata
Filled with murderous attacks, fatal stratagems and cutthroat tactics, a special section tests the reader while analyzing in depth a classic game by the master himself.

Intermediate Level Power Builder, Vol. 1, by Wang RuNan 8 dan
The book is based on a Chinese television program about go hosted by Wang RuNan 8 dan. The book emphasizes basic concepts, theories, and techniques for intermediate level players. This volume covers openings and invasions useful for Kyu-level as well as low dan level players.

Igo Hatsuyo-ron - Volume I by Dosetsu Inseki
Hailed as the highest authority in life and death problems, it contains 183 problems. Volume I contains the first 63 problems. Of all the life & death problem books in the literature, none exceeds the level of Igo Hatsuyo-ron. It sets the line between amateur and professional players.

Master Go In Ten Days by Xu Xiang and Jin Jiang
The book is designed to help beginners reach three or two kyu level amateur strength.

Nie Weiping On Go by Nie Weiping
Using positions from his own games, one of the finest Chinese players shows how a grasp of full board principles is essential for effective play. Tactics in all phases of the game, as well as the operation of thickness is covered.

100 Challenging Go Problems for 100 Days of Study by The Nihon Kiin
Test your skill and develop a disciplined study regimen at the sairne time. This book is filled with such a wide variety of refined tactics and insights into strategy, reading and perception, that many more than I 00 days of enjoyment can be anticipated.

Pro-Pro Handicap Go by the Nihon Kiin
Subtitled "Invincible Play with 3, 4 and 5 Stones," this book is designed to teach you how to get the most out of handicap stones. Model play is highly illustrated with black getting full handicap value. All games are analyzed in terms that weaker players can easily understand, and tests are included to measure the reader's real strength. A thoroughly enjoyable book to read!

Proverbs, Vol. 1, Nihon Ki-in Handbook Series
This book collects and explains over a hundred fifty proverbs that have arisen over the centuries to help players remember various aspects of the game. There are eleven chapters: Basic Moves and Concepts; Good Shape and Bad; Playing Ko; The Opening; Joseki; Territorial Frameworks; Life and Death; Running, Connecting, and Capturing; Clever Moves, Forcing Moves, and Sacrifices; A Guide to Fighting; and a Potpourri of Proverbs.

Strategic Fundamentals in Go, by Guo Tisheng
Ten important lessons are discussed in detail, namely, sente vs. gote, big vs. small points, attack vs. defense, life vs. death, big vs. small territories, saving vs. sacrificing stones, light vs. heavy shapes, slack moves vs. urgent points, standard moves vs. flexible variations, persistence vs. playing safe. With the aid of many illustrations, this book helps the reader to master these issues and thus become a stronger player.

Tesuji and Anti-Suji of Go by Sakata Eio
The follow-up book to Killer of Go. If you want to emulate the exemplary play shown in Killer of Go, you have to understand how to exploit the potential for skilled play (tesuji), as well as to recognize crude play (anti-suji). 224 pages with glossary and index.

The Thirty Six Stratagems Applied to Go by Ma Xiaochun
Ranked as the best player in the world in 1995, Ma Xiaochun has a
phenomena] career since turning professional just ten years ago.
This book represents his first major work of Go literature. It
examines the application of ancient military maxims to the game of
Go.

Utilizing Outward Influence by Jin Jiang and Zhao Zheng
Provides a study of how to efficiently build and use outward
influence. Numerous examples of how to construct thickness and
avoid thinness are given. Includes numerous examples for
constructing thickness or outward influence through pivot point,
sacrifice, and ko tactics.

Winning A Won Game, Vol. 2, Go Seigen Series
Go Seigen provides Three Golden Rules with examples of their
application in actual games. One often encounters professional
games lost after building up a commanding lead, or a game won by
turning the tables on the opponent. This book highlights such
cases.

Yang Yilun's Ingenious Life and Death Puzzles- Volume 1
and 2
A collection of over 200 life-and-death problems in each volume
designed by Sensei Yang known as "yly" and "rabcat" on the
Internet Go Server (IGS). By studying these intriguing puzzles one
can greatly improve one's reading/fighting abilities and appreciate
the beauty of Go.

**Yutopian Enterprises, 2255 29th Street, Santa Monica, CA
90405, USA**
Web: http://www.yutopian.com
E-mail: Sales@yutopian.com
Tel: 1-800-988-6463 or 1-310-578-7181
Fax: 1-310-578-7381